# KNOW YOUR INVISIBLE ENEMIES

## ... and defeat them

## Dag Heward-Mills

## Parchment House

**KNOW YOUR INVISIBLE ENEMIES**
**... AND DEFEAT THEM**

First published 2017 by Parchment House
4th Printing 2020

[77]Find out more about Dag Heward-Mills at:

Healing Jesus Campaign
Email: evangelist@daghewardmills.org
Website: www.daghewardmills.org
Facebook: Dag Heward-Mills
Twitter: @EvangelistDag

ISBN : 978-1-68398-264-7

# *Contents*

# CHAPTER 1

# The List of Invisible Enemies

The Bible gives us a good list of invisible enemies. It is our duty to believe the Word of God and fight every single one of them until we crush them under our feet. Do not under-estimate the reality of the spirit world. The spirit world is the real world. This world is the temporary (unreal) world. Here is a list of invisible enemies you must expect to encounter while you live on this earth. Jesus Christ did not go far before He encountered devils. He encountered devils throughout His life and ministry on this earth.

1. **Principalities are invisible enemies.**

    For we wrestle not against flesh and blood, but against principalities, against powers, against the rulers of the darkness of this world, against spiritual wickedness in high places.

    Ephesians 6:12

2. **Powers are invisible enemies.**

    For we wrestle not against flesh and blood, but against principalities, against powers, against the rulers of the darkness of this world, against spiritual wickedness in high places.

Ephesians 6:12

## 3. Rulers of Spiritual Darkness are invisible enemies.

For we wrestle not against flesh and blood, but against principalities, against powers, against the rulers of the darkness of this world, against spiritual wickedness in high places.

Ephesians 6:12

## 4. Spiritual Wickedness is an invisible enemy.

For we wrestle not against flesh and blood, but against principalities, against powers, against the rulers of the darkness of this world, against spiritual wickedness in high places.

Ephesians 6:12

## 5. Unclean Spirits are invisible enemies.

And they were all amazed, and spake among themselves, saying, what a word is this! For with authority and power he commandeth the UNCLEAN SPIRITS, and they come out.

Luke 4:36

And when he had called unto him his twelve disciples, he gave them power against UNCLEAN SPIRITS, to cast them out, and to heal all manner of sickness and all manner of disease.

Matthew 10:1

## 6. Foul Spirits are invisible enemies.

When Jesus saw that the people came running together, he rebuked the FOUL SPIRIT, saying unto him, thou dumb and deaf spirit, I charge thee, come out of him, and enter no more into him.

Mark 9:25

### 7.    Fallen Angels are invisible enemies.

And THE ANGELS WHICH KEPT NOT THEIR FIRST ESTATE, but left their own habitation, he hath reserved in everlasting chains under darkness unto the judgment of the great day.

Jude 1:6

### 8.    Princes of this World are invisible enemies.

Which none of the PRINCES OF THIS WORLD knew: for had they known it, they would not have crucified the Lord of glory.

1 Corinthians 2:8

### 9.    Demons are invisible enemies.

They drove out many DEMONS and anointed many sick people with oil and healed them.

Mark 6:13 (NIV)

### 10.    Thrones are invisible enemies.

For by him were all things created, that are in heaven, and that are in earth, visible and invisible, whether they be THRONES, or dominions, or principalities, or powers: all things were created by him, and for him:

Colossians 1:16

### 11.    Dominions are invisible enemies.

For by him were all things created, that are in heaven, and that are in earth, visible and invisible, whether they be thrones, or DOMINIONS, or principalities, or powers: all things were created by him, and for him:

Colossians 1:16

## 12.  Spiritual Flies and Insects are invisible enemies.

And the scribes which came down from Jerusalem said, He hath BEELZEBUB, and by the prince of the devils casteth he out devils.

And he called them unto him, and said unto them in parables, how can Satan cast out Satan? And if a kingdom be divided against itself, that kingdom cannot stand.

Mark 3:22-24

## 13.  Hateful Spiritual Birds are invisible enemies.  Some demons are referred to as hateful birds.

And he cried mightily with a strong voice, saying, Babylon the great is fallen, is fallen, and is become the habitation of devils, and the hold of every foul spirit, and a cage of EVERY UNCLEAN AND HATEFUL BIRD.

Revelation 18:2

## 14.  Frog Spirits are invisible enemies.  Some demons are referred to as frogs.

And I saw three UNCLEAN SPIRITS LIKE FROGS come out of the mouth of the dragon, and out of the mouth of the beast, and out of the mouth of the false prophet. For they are the spirits of devils, working miracles, which go forth unto the kings of the earth and of the whole world, to gather them to the battle of that great day of God Almighty.

Revelation 16:13-14

## 15.  Spiritual Scorpions are invisible enemies:  Some evil spirits are referred to as scorpions.

Behold, I give unto you power to tread on serpents and SCORPIONS, and over all the power of the enemy: and nothing shall by any means hurt you.

Luke 10:19

16. **Spiritual Dragons are invisible enemies:** Some evil spirits are referred to as dragons.

And THE GREAT DRAGON WAS CAST OUT, that old serpent, called the Devil, and Satan, which deceiveth the whole world: he was cast out into the earth, and his angels were cast out with him.

Revelation 12:9

17. **Spiritual Snakes are invisible enemies:** Some evil spirits are referred to as serpents. Obviously, these are not physical snakes but spiritual snakes.

And THE SERPENT cast out of his mouth water as a flood after the woman, that he might cause her to be carried away of the flood.

Revelations 12:15

18. **Spiritual Horses and their Riders are invisible enemies**

And I looked, and behold a pale horse: and his name that sat on him was Death, and Hell followed with him. And power was given unto them over the fourth part of the earth, to kill with sword, and with hunger, and with death, and with the beasts of the earth.

Revelation 6:8

19. **Spiritual Sea Monsters are invisible enemies.** Some evil spirits are referred to as Leviathan. Leviathan is a well-known sea monster or sea creature with many heads.

Thou brakest the heads of LEVIATHAN in pieces, and gavest him to be meat to the people inhabiting the wilderness.

Psalms 74:14

20. **Multiple-headed Monsters in the sea are in the list of invisible enemies.** Some demons are multiple-headed monsters living in the sea. Some call these marine spirits.

> And I stood upon the sand of the sea, and saw A BEAST RISE UP OUT OF THE SEA, having seven heads and ten horns, and upon his horns ten crowns, and upon his heads the name of blasphemy.
>
> Revelation 13:1

21. **Monsters from under the earth are in the list of invisible enemies.** Some demons are monsters in the earth. These are terrestrial spirits.

> And I beheld ANOTHER BEAST COMING UP OUT OF THE EARTH; and he had two horns like a lamb, and he spake as a dragon.
>
> Revelation 13:11

# CHAPTER 2

# The Ten Assignments of Demons Against You

For a great door and effectual is opened unto me, and there are MANY ADVERSARIES.

1 Corinthians 16:9

# No "Calling" Goes Unopposed

Thee is no commission or calling that goes without opposition. If God calls you, you will be opposed by the devil. Satan will fight you, because that is all he is there for. Every great calling goes with great opposition.

For a great door and effectual is opened unto me, and there are many adversaries.

1 Corinthians 16:9

When Moses was called to set the Israelites free, he was met with great opposition from Pharaoh. Pharaoh is a type of satan who will not let God's people go. Pharaoh represents the devil who hates the idea of people serving God. All male Israelite children were slaughtered in an attempt to eliminate Moses from this world.

When Jesus was born into this world to save mankind he met with Herod who ordered the slaughter of all children in an attempt to eliminate the Saviour. The great call and commission of Jesus as the Saviour of this world was met with the highest kind of resistance.

Your calling will equally be met with fierce resistance. All the creatures mentioned in the previous chapter will gang up against you to make sure that you do not finish your call. If you insist on working for God, you will be resisted, frustrated, accused, harassed and opposed by an invisible enemy all through your life and ministry. If you do not pray, and if you are not spiritual, you will not last in this fierce invisible war. Demons are real. Evil creatures are real. It is time to find out exactly what you are dealing with and crush it.

## Your Destiny Depends on Crushing the Enemy With Power

Without the power of God you will not fulfil your calling. The scripture is clear; you receive all things that are given to you through the power of God. The power of God is the channel through which we receive many things we need. The power of God is necessary to crush the adversary. The enemy understands the language of power.

**According as HIS DIVINE POWER HATH GIVEN UNTO US all things that pertain unto life and godliness, through the knowledge of him that hath called us to glory and virtue:**

**2 Peter 1:3**

## Ten Assignments of Demons Against You

### 1.   RESISTANCE AND OPPOSITION

Be sober, be vigilant; because your ADVERSARY the devil, as a roaring lion, walketh about, seeking whom he may devour:

1 Peter 5:8

Your adversaries are resisting the idea of you becoming anything important. All forms of resistance that you feel as you attempt to obey the will of God, are caused by the many adversaries. I have felt resistance from all quarters since I began my ministry.

Sometimes the resistance is from the world out there, but sometimes it is from my bishops; sometimes it is from my helpers; sometimes it is from my family. Whatever the case, you must identify resistance as demonic.

Be sober, be vigilant; because YOUR ADVERSARY the devil, as a roaring lion, walketh about, seeking whom he may devour:

1 Peter 5:8

An adversary is someone who opposes, obstructs, prevents and stops you from achieving what you have set out to accomplish.

When you think of the words opposition, frustration, difficulties, delays, think of demons. Think of satanic activities whenever you are experiencing delays, frustration and obstructions to your calling.

Many frustrations in the ministry are caused by demons. No matter how beautiful things look on the outside, evil spirits are present. Evil spirits are present to oppose, frustrate and fight God's servants.

Many of the difficulties and challenges that a minister experiences, are caused by evil spirits. The more spiritual you become, the more conscious you will be of the activity of evil spirits.

## 2.  FRUSTRATION

And he shall speak great words against the most High, and shall WEAR OUT THE SAINTS of the most High, and think to change times and laws: and they shall be given into his hand until a time and times and the dividing of time.

Daniel 7:25

As part of the plans to oppose you, satan sets out to frustrate you. Every kind of irritation, disturbance and annoyance that you experience are all signs of demonic activity. Sometimes, the irritation and annoyance come from internal issues. A simple job can drag on and becomes a long and unpleasant experience. It is the constant presence of devils sent out to oppose and frustrate the work of God that leads to this kind of experience.

## 3.  BLOCKING PEOPLE

From that time forth began Jesus to shew unto his disciples, how that he must go unto Jerusalem, and suffer many things of the elders and chief priests and scribes, and be killed, and be raised again the third day. Then Peter took him, and began to rebuke him, saying, be it far from thee, Lord: THIS SHALL NOT BE UNTO THEE.

Matthew 16:21-22

Stopping the work of the Lord entirely is one of satan's happiest occasions. It means he has been able to go further in his effort to frustrate the work of God. He has been able to stop it completely on many occasions. Watch out for things that bring the work of God to a complete halt.

## 4.    TEMPTING PEOPLE

And immediately the Spirit driveth him into the wilderness. And he was there in the wilderness forty days, tempted of Satan; and was with the wild beasts; and the angels ministered unto him.

Mark 1:12-13

Tempting and testing God's people as they work for the Lord is the work of devils. Most men of God are under constant temptation as they serve God. Many people trip up on unforgiveness, lust, impatience and other temptations.

## 5.    FRIGHTENING PEOPLE

Be sober, be vigilant; because your adversary the devil, as a roaring lion, walketh about, seeking whom he may devour:

1 Peter 5:8

All forms of fear are from the devil. Many men and women are completely controlled by their fears. Fear is an influencing and guiding spirit. It seeks to guide you and lead you along a path that ends with you hitting your head against a wall.

## 6.    CHARMING PEOPLE

But I fear, lest by any means, as the serpent beguiled Eve through his subtilty, so your minds should be corrupted from the simplicity that is in Christ.

2 Corinthians 11:3

And the great dragon was cast out, that old serpent, called the Devil, and Satan, which deceiveth the whole world: he was cast out into the earth, and his angels were cast out with him.

Revelation 12:9

Satan is well known to poison the hearts of Christians. Many are poisoned with mistrust, bitterness, treachery, disloyalty and confusion. Accusations are one of the most deadly poisons that can be thrown into the hearts of Christians. Many people lose their innocence because satan drops some of his poison into their hearts. When you meet a group of people who are so affected by things they have experienced, they are probably poisoned by the devil.

## 7.    DECEPTION

Ye are of your father the devil, and the lusts of your father ye will do. He was a murderer from the beginning, and abode not in the truth, because there is no truth in him. When he speaketh a lie, he speaketh of his own: for he is a liar, and the father of it.

John 8:44

Lying and deception are activities of devils. Whenever you meet a liar you encounter great frustrations. A liar is usually a thief and is taking something away from you. People who tell half-truths and people who mislead are all sent by satan to frustrate you and destroy you. Throughout your life and ministry you will encounter such people. They are all agents of the devil, sent to destroy you.

Every minister of the gospel must watch out for something or someone trying to deceive him. Satan is always trying to misdirect you, mislead you, distract you and misinform you. He is always trying to hide something from you and make you walk in darkness, ignorance and deception. This is the constant and unchanging work of evil spirits. This is why you must constantly pray for wisdom, understanding, knowledge, counsel, light and revelation. Daniel was seen as someone who had been delivered from the darkness of deception. He was described as someone with light, understanding and wisdom. Because of the light, understanding and wisdom that he had, he was chosen and appointed by the king. He was called for because he had broken through the darkness and received light and revelation from God. Those who are more powerful, are those who overcome the darkness in the world and have received light.

THERE IS A MAN IN THY KINGDOM, in whom is the spirit of the holy gods; and in the days of thy father LIGHT and UNDERSTANDING and WISDOM, like the wisdom of the gods, was found in him; whom the king Nebuchadnezzar thy father, the king, I say, thy father, made master of the magicians, astrologers, Chaldeans, and soothsayers;

Forasmuch as an excellent spirit, and knowledge, and understanding, interpreting of dreams, and shewing of hard sentences, and dissolving of doubts, were found in the same Daniel, whom the king named Belteshazzar: NOW LET DANIEL BE CALLED, and he will shew the interpretation.

Daniel 5:11-12

And the great dragon was cast out, that old serpent, called the Devil, and Satan, which deceiveth the whole world: he was cast out into the earth, and his angels were cast out with him.

Revelation 12:9

## 8.  STEALING

The thief cometh not, but for TO STEAL, and to kill, and to destroy: I am come that they might have life, and that they might have it more abundantly.

John 10:10

Stealing money, taking away what does not belong to you is one of the top activities of demons and evil spirits. Anytime someone is robbed, an attack of demonic frustrations and demonic setbacks is unleashed against him. You need to control all forms of stealing that take place around your life in order to stifle the activity of devils in and around you.

## 9.    BETRAYAL AND DISLOYALTY

And supper being ended, the devil having now put into the heart of Judas Iscariot, Simon's son, to betray him;

John 13:2

Wherever relationships are destroyed, devils have been working hard. They are successful when they are able to divide good friends and happy couples. Destruction of churches is the work of devils. Jesus is building the church and the devils are trying to destroy it. All ministries that have been brought down by corruption and fornication were really brought down by devils. You may have seen some physical people working out the corruption and immorality. However, the real deal is that a host of devils are at work.

## 10.    KILLING

The thief cometh not, but for to steal, and TO KILL, and to destroy: I am come that they might have life, and that they might have it more abundantly.

John 10:10

The death of Jesus Christ was orchestrated by devils. All forms of stealing, killing and destroying are from the devil. Satan is a murderer and his ultimate aim is to kill all of us. Given the chance, he will inflict diseases, accidents and tragedies on every single one of us. Every disease, every setback and every tragedy that occurs is demonically orchestrated to oppose and frustrate the work of God.

# CHAPTER 3

# Special Targets of the Invisible Enemy

And Jesus being full of the Holy Ghost returned from Jordan, and was led by the Spirit into the wilderness,

Being forty days tempted of the devil. And in those days he did eat nothing: and when they were ended, he afterward hungered.

**Luke 4:1-2**

I n the ministry of Jesus, we see those who were specially targeted by devils. It is interesting to see where Jesus encountered devils whilst He ministered. Surprisingly, Jesus encountered devils in church and in religious circles. He also encountered devils at the highest level of leadership. You would have thought that He would have found devils mostly in drinking bars and centres of prostitution. Amazingly, most of the devils were found in church and with church people. It is no surprise that as Jesus was being crucified by the pastors and priests of Jerusalem, the armed robbers, the prostitutes and the drunkards were sleeping peacefully in their beds. Indeed, many devils can be found in the church and among church people. Satan already controls worldly people. It is important to recognize that we, the church, are his special targets.

1.    **In the ministry of Jesus, CHURCH MEMBERS were specially targeted by devils.**

And there was in their synagogue a man with an unclean spirit; and he cried out, Saying, Let us alone; what have we to do with thee, thou Jesus of Nazareth? Art thou come to destroy us? I know thee who thou art, the Holy One of God. And Jesus rebuked him, saying, Hold thy peace, and come out of him.

Mark 1:23-25

Jesus encountered evil spirits in the synagogue. Jesus Christ encountered devils in church members. Some of the church members screamed whilst He preached because of the presence of evil spirits. Other evil spirits make people roll around on the floor, screaming and shaking helplessly.

And they brought the boy to Him. And when he saw Him, immediately the spirit threw him into a convulsion, and falling to the ground, he began rolling about and foaming at the mouth.

Mark 9:20, NASB

Devils are also the cause of many kinds of evil that occur around you. Demons caused fires, armed robberies, thefts and deaths to Job and his family. Evil spirits are the real cause of many evils in our lives. To live your life on this earth and pretend that these things are not there is to sell yourself into the hands of the enemy.

## 2. In the ministry of Jesus, RELIGIOUS AND CHURCH LEADERS were specially targeted by demons.

Ye are of your father the devil, and the lusts of your father ye will do. He was a murderer from the beginning, and abode not in the truth, because there is no truth in him. When he speaketh a lie, he speaketh of his own: for he is a liar, and the father of it.

John 8:44

Satan loves to invade the church and its leadership. Jesus pointed out to the Pharisees that they were under the influence of the devil. The fact that they were religious leaders did not confuse Jesus. The fact that the Pharisees were senior men of the house of God did not confuse or deceive Jesus Christ. When Peter was appointed as the head of the church he was immediately attacked by the devil. Jesus saw through Peter when he spoke against the cross. He knew the devil had invaded the newly appointed religious leader. It is sad to see how evil spirits have invaded the lives of many religious leaders. When you receive a promotion from the Lord, you must expect an attack from the devil.

And Jesus answered and said unto him, Blessed art thou, Simon Barjona: for flesh and blood hath not revealed it unto thee, but my Father which is in heaven. And I say also unto thee, That THOU ART PETER, AND UPON THIS ROCK I WILL BUILD MY CHURCH; and the gates of hell shall not prevail against it.

And I will give unto thee the keys of the kingdom of heaven: and whatsoever thou shalt bind on earth shall be bound in heaven: and whatsoever thou shalt loose on earth shall be loosed in heaven. Then charged he his disciples that they should tell no man that he was Jesus the Christ.

From that time forth began Jesus to shew unto his disciples, how that he must go unto Jerusalem, and suffer many things of the elders and chief priests and scribes, and be killed, and be raised again the third day.

Then Peter took him, and began to rebuke him, saying, Be it far from thee, Lord: this shall not be unto thee.

But he turned, and said unto Peter, GET THEE BEHIND ME, SATAN: thou art an offence unto me: for thou savourest not the things that be of God, but those that be of men.

Matthew 16:17-23

Develop the gift of discernment! Become like Jesus! Be able to see through the religious façade and the hypocrisies of spiritual leaders.

### 3. In the ministry of Jesus, CLOSE ASSOCIATES were targeted by demons.

Then Peter took him, and began to rebuke him, saying, be it far from thee, Lord: this shall not be unto thee. But he turned, and said unto Peter, Get thee behind me, Satan: thou art an offence unto me: for thou savourest not the things that be of God, but those that be of men.

Matthew 16:22-23

Fallen angels, devils and other evil spirits love to attack close associates. Jesus identified the devil in Peter. Satan invaded Judas.

And after the sop SATAN ENTERED INTO HIM. Then said Jesus unto him, That thou doest, do quickly.

John 13:27

You will also need to identify the devil in the "Peters" and the "Judases" of your life. Peter's closeness to Jesus as well as his strategic positioning made him a strong target for the devil. In your own life and ministry, you will have a "Peter". This "Peter" could be an associate or assistant pastor or friend. It will take a great deal of understanding and knowledge about the devil to be able to identify the devil when he speaks through your closest and most trusted associate and friend. Will you be able to identify Judas when satan enters into him? Will you know when an evil spirit has invaded one of your close associates?

**4.    In the ministry of Jesus, BEST FRIENDS AND ASSISTANTS were targeted by demons.**

When Jesus identified the devil in Peter, He was also identifying someone who was very close and familiar with Him. In your life today, the closest and most familiar person to you may be your wife. Many ministers' wives are targets for demons. Many ministers struggle with their wives, thinking they are struggling with marital challenges. They often do not realise that they are in direct conflict with satan or a fallen angel.

Then Peter took him, and began to rebuke him, saying, be it far from thee, Lord: this shall not be unto thee.

But he turned, and said unto Peter, Get thee behind me, Satan: thou art an offence unto me: for thou savourest not the things that be of God, but those that be of men.

Matthew 16:22-23

# CHAPTER 4

# The Five Realms of Operation of Evil Spirits

## 1. DEMONS OPERATE IN THE INVISIBLE WORLD.

There is an invisible world out there. In that invisible world, there are angels, demons, fallen angels, hybrid creatures, thrones, dominions, principalities, powers, wicked spirits and a host of spiritual animals. Moses prevailed because he dealt with the invisible world.

> **By faith he forsook Egypt, not fearing the wrath of the king: for he endured, as SEEING HIM WHO IS INVISIBLE.**
>
> **Hebrews 11:27**

In a war with an invisible enemy, you must make special efforts to know and understand your enemy. Many years ago, I was listening to a teaching by Kenneth Hagin on demonology. He was explaining how evil spirits affect Christians today. He explained a vision in which he saw an imp-like figure sitting on the shoulders of a pastor's wife and ministering thoughts and ideas to her. He shared how this lady began to enjoy and accept those thoughts until the spirit moved into her head and down into her heart. This lady, now fully under the influence of the demon, left her husband and went out into the world. She committed adultery with several different men until she finally renounced Christ. He explained how the Lord showed the process that led to this woman being captured by the enemy. This story resonated in my spirit and I became much more aware of the activities taking place in the dark world.

Do not think you know everything. You will discover that many things you struggle with are demonic in nature. Make special efforts to know every detail about your enemy.

## 2.    DEMONS OPERATE IN THE SPIRIT REALM.

**For he that speaketh in an unknown tongue speaketh not unto men, but unto God: for no man understandeth him; howbeit IN THE SPIRIT he speaketh mysteries.**

**1 Corinthians 14:2**

Paul speaks of the spirit realm when he teaches about praying in tongues. He explains that speaking in tongues is about operating in the spirit. He says that in the spirit he speaks mysteries. He does not speak mysteries in the flesh. This is why tongues is feared so much by devils. Speaking in tongues puts you directly into the spirit realm where the demons are.

The spirit realm contains the spirits. Flesh and blood do not operate in that realm. A good Christian must graduate from fighting with flesh and blood to fighting in the spirit realm. Paul said, "We do not war after the flesh. We do not wrestle against flesh and blood." If we do not wrestle with flesh and blood, we wrestle with the spirits.

**For we wrestle NOT AGAINST FLESH AND BLOOD, but against principalities, against powers, against the rulers of the darkness of this world, against spiritual wickedness in high places.**

**Ephesians 6:12**

**For though we walk in the flesh, we do NOT WAR AFTER THE FLESH:**

**2 Corinthians 10:3**

## 3.  DEMONS OPERATE IN THE REALM OF DARKNESS.

There is a dark world out there.  There is a realm called "spiritual darkness".  A Christian must make special efforts to know about evil creatures, evil spirits and their activities.  There are many creatures that are imprisoned in that dark realm.  That is where they operate.  Their operations in that realm affect us greatly.

**And the angels which kept not their first estate, but left their own habitation, he hath reserved IN EVERLASTING CHAINS UNDER DARKNESS unto the judgment of the great day.**

**Jude 6**

Even from that imprisoned realm of darkness, these evil creatures are fighting against us.  There are creatures called "the rulers of the darkness" (Ephesians 6:12).  These are creatures that rule other creatures in the dark world.  These creatures rule and dominate in the darkness.  Indeed, salvation begins when you are set free from the powers that reside in darkness.

**Who hath delivered us from the POWER OF DARKNESS, and hath translated us into the kingdom of his dear Son:**

**Colossians 1:13**

## 4.  DEMONS OPERATE FROM THE DARK PLACES OF THE EARTH.

**Have respect unto the covenant: for THE DARK PLACES OF THE EARTH ARE FULL OF THE HABITATIONS OF CRUELTY.**

**Psalm 74:20**

There are parts of the earth that are dominated by evil. These places are the launching pads of demon activity. Demonic ideas are exported to the rest of the world from such places. The dark places of the earth are the places where evil is practiced. Wickedness rules and evil prevails in the dark places of the earth. When the preaching of the Word of God comes to such a dark place, the people who live there simply cannot understand it. Jesus knew about this and predicted it. He said, "This is the condemnation, that light has come into the world but men love the darkness so much more than the light."

**And the light shineth in darkness; and the darkness comprehended it not.**

**John 1:5**

**And this is the condemnation, that light is come into the world, and men loved darkness rather than light, because their deeds were evil. For every one that doeth evil hateth the light, neither cometh to the light, lest his deeds should be reproved.**

**John 3:19-20**

## 5.    DEMONS OPERATE IN THE NIGHT.

**Ye are all the children of light, and the children of the day: WE ARE NOT OF THE NIGHT, nor of darkness.**

**1 Thessalonians 5:5**

**But WHILE MEN SLEPT, his enemy came and sowed tares among the wheat, and went his way. But when the blade was sprung up, and brought forth fruit, then appeared the tares also. So the servants of the householder came and said unto him, Sir, didst not thou sow good seed in thy field? From whence then hath it tares? He said unto them, an enemy hath done this. The servants said unto him, Wilt thou then that we go and gather them up?**

**Matthew 13:25-28**

The "night" is another situation referred to by Paul. This is the absence of day. When night falls, evil sprouts. Most thieves wait for the evening to get to work. They simply cannot operate in the day. Most of the sins in our world take place at night and in the darkness. This is the time when men sleep. Whenever men take their rest and decide to relax, night has fallen and satan gets to work. Be careful in your moments of relaxation and rest because this is the time evil spirits get to work.

# CHAPTER 5

# Symptoms of Demon Presence

And they asked him, saying, Master, but when shall these things be? And WHAT SIGN WILL THERE BE ...?

**Luke 21:7**

**F**ighting the devil is to fight an invisible enemy! Detecting the presence and activities of evil spirits is key to being a successful Christian. A minister of the gospel must be even more capable of detecting the presence and activities of evil spirits. If you are able to detect, isolate and destroy your enemy, you will overcome him.

Fighting the devil is to fight an invisible enemy. Fighting an invisible enemy is not as impossible as it sounds. Doctors have been doing that for years! Fighting devils is similar to the work of a doctor because doctors fight invisible bacteria, parasites and viruses all the time.

Doctors have been forced to fight invisible enemies for years. After years of experience, medical doctors are able to detect, isolate and deal with their invisible enemies.

A minister of the gospel must be like a good doctor. You must grow in your spiritual walk until you are quickly able to detect the presence of evil spirits. Very few people have visions and revelations in which they see devils and demons at work. Many doctors have also never seen certain viruses or bacteria but they are able to fight them effectively.

You do not have to see your enemy in order to defeat him! But you do have to know when your enemy is present! You do have to know what exactly he is doing! You do have to know how your enemy operates! It is possible to detect the presence of an invisible enemy through symptoms and signs.

There are several symptoms of demonic activity. Every minister of the gospel must know them because it is the only way to detect demon activity. The symptoms and patterns of disease are well known to doctors. If a person has night sweats, weight loss and a chronic cough, most doctors would immediately think of tuberculosis. Why? Because symptoms are repeated each time the bacteria is present. If a person lives in West Africa and has a headache, fever, feels cold followed by a hot feeling with sweating, most doctors would think of malaria. You cannot see the malaria parasite, but you know it must be present somewhere.

If the fever goes down only to resurface after forty-eight hours, you would think even more of malaria because the parasites multiply and are released from the liver into the body in a forty-eight hour cycle.

If a child has shortness of breath, fatigue with a little physical activity, blue lips and a blue tongue, many doctors would think of a congenital heart disease. Just as doctors know patterns of symptoms, Christians must know symptoms and patterns of demonic activity.

**Then answered the Jews, and said unto him, Say we not well that thou art a Samaritan, and hast a devil? Jesus answered, I HAVE NOT A DEVIL; but I honour my Father, and ye do dishonour me.**

**John 8:48-49**

Human beings have always sought for ways to uncover devils. Christians sometimes level accusations at each other and say, "You have a devil." "That brother is demonized!" "That sister is demon-possessed!" "My husband is possessed!" "My wife has a devil in her!" These are statements that are often made by Christians. But are they really accurate?

Devils are like mice and rats. They live amongst us. They eat our food. They destroy our property and they make us feel uncomfortable. But they constantly run away into darkness and hide from us. It is, however, possible to detect their presence by the tell-tale signs they leave behind. Unfortunately, the Pharisees accused Jesus of having a devil. They accused him of harbouring a demon and operating by that demon power. This is not an unusual accusation for a man of God. But it is unfortunate that such an accusation should be levelled against the Saviour of the world. If you are a servant of God, do not expect anything better.

Jesus, however, vehemently rejected the accusation that He had a devil. He pointed out to them that He honoured His father and therefore could not have a devil. People who have devils in them do not honour fathers. There is no need to make mistakes when you are trying to locate devils. There are clear symptoms and signs you must know if you are to detect the presence of devils. Honouring the father is definitely not the sign of the presence of a devil.

## Symptoms of Demon Presence

**And the great dragon was cast out, that old serpent, CALLED THE DEVIL, AND SATAN, which deceiveth the whole world: he was cast out into the earth, and his angels were cast out with him.**

**Revelation 12:9**

The easiest way to identify symptoms of demonic activity is to use the names and titles given to the devil in the Bible. You must watch out for occurrences that bring any of the names of satan to your mind. Names and titles are often given to describe a person. For instance, if someone is called the "king of Pop music" it reveals a lot about what he actually does. You can expect him to be found where pop music is found. You can also expect to see him anywhere pop music is being played. If someone is called the "king of Reggae music", you can expect to see him or his associates wherever reggae music is being played. You can expect to find his influence anywhere reggae music is being played.

Satan has many names. Each of the names of satan describes a particular kind of activity. Each of the names of satan shows you the symptoms and patterns that will be created by demonic presence. A minister of the gospel must watch out for occurrences that bring any of the names of satan to mind. By knowing the names of satan, you will become conscious of any activity which points to him.

1.   **The symptom of lying and deception.**

**Satan is called a liar and the father of lies: Watch out for THE SYMPTOM OF LYING AND DECEPTION.** "Ye are of your father the devil... When he speaketh a lie, he speaketh of his own: for he is a liar, and the father of it" (John 8:44). Where there is a lot of lying and deception, there is a lot of demonic activity.

Watch out for countries that have a lot of lying and deception! These countries have a proliferation of demons. Do you know any countries where the people constantly tell lies and deceive one another?

I once visited a nation for a crusade. This country is well known for lying and deceit. In the night, I experienced unusual demonic attacks which I have never experienced in any other country. I was surprised because this was a country that was also well known for Christian activity. But the scripture was being confirmed. A lot of lying and a lot of deception go along with a lot of demonic activity.

Watch out for jobs which involve a lot of lying and deception! Do you know any jobs where people have to tell a lot of lies and deceive people? Such jobs will always have a lot of demonic activity associated with them! Unfortunately, politics has often involved telling lies and deceiving the people. This need not be the case, but many politicians feel that they have to lie in order to win votes. Hordes of demons are known to flood into the work of politics, as everyone tries to deceive the other. Christians must be very careful when they venture into that realm.

## 2. The symptom of murder.

**Satan is called a murderer: Watch out for THE SYMPTOM OF MURDER.** "Ye are of your father the devil … He was a murderer from the beginning, and abode not in the truth, because there is no truth in him…" (John 8:44).

Watch out for nations which have a high murder rate! There is a lot of demon activity in those countries.

Watch out for those who kill a lot of people!

Watch out for those who shamelessly and violently cause the deaths of innocent people!

Watch out for heartless murderers who kill, maim and destroy without reason! These unreasonable actions reveal nothing else but the presence of satan.

Where there are persistent and unusual murders, you must immediately think of the devil. When you hear of people being murdered senselessly, beheaded, tortured, etc, you must think of the presence of devils. There have been many wars and revolutions that resulted in senseless killing of people. For instance, the Second World War was a senseless conflict that led to the deaths of fifty million people. The inexplicable destruction that was released on the world through this war reveals a clear presence of active devils.

## 3.  The symptom of accusation.

**Satan is called the accuser of the brethren:  Watch out for THE SYMPTOM OF ACCUSATION in your life and ministry.** "And I heard a loud voice saying in heaven, Now is come salvation, and strength, and the kingdom of our God, and the power of his Christ: for the accuser of our brethren is cast down, which accused them before our God day and night" (Revelation 12:10). Where there are persistent and unusual accusations, you must immediately think of satanic activity! Are you experiencing persistent accusations about anything? You are probably experiencing satanic activity!

## 4.  The symptom of opposition.

**Satan is called the adversary:  Watch out for THE SYMPTOM OF OPPOSITION to your ministry.** "Be sober, be vigilant; because your adversary the devil, as a roaring lion, walketh about, seeking whom he may devour" (1 Peter 5:8). Where there is persistent and unusual opposition to your life and ministry, you must immediately think of the devil. The opposing forces and people that hinder you are inspired by satan himself. Most ministers of the gospel have an opposing spirit sent to fight against them. These opposing spirits slow them down and make things very difficult for them. Watch out for opposition, difficulty, slowness and hindrances to your ministry. Many of the things that slow you down are demonic in origin. People who fight and oppose you are often inspired by the devil.

## 5.    The symptom of temptation.

**Satan is called the tempter:    Watch out for THE SYMPTOM OF TEMPTATIONS.** "And when the tempter came to him, he said, If thou be the Son of God, command that these stones be made bread" (Matthew 4:3). Where there are persistent and unusual temptations in your life, you must think of demonic activity. Temptations are orchestrated by the devil. Satan is behind many of the people that come into your life to tempt and test you.

## 6.    The symptom of disloyalty.

**Jesus answered them, Have not I chosen you twelve, and ONE OF YOU IS A DEVIL?**

**John 6:70**

Judas Iscariot was disloyal to Jesus Christ, his Lord and master. Treachery is extreme disloyalty. Wherever you have disloyal and unfaithful people, you will have demonic activity. Demons invade churches and destroy them through disloyalty and treachery. Where members criticise their leader and undermine their pastors all the time there are demons in plentiful supply. Where there are criticisms, accusations, murmuring, rumours and fault-finding, there are lots of demons at work. Many pastors in their ignorance do not recognize that demons are in full operation through murmurers, fault-finders, critics and accusers. They think the people have a bad attitude. Jesus said, "One of you is a devil". In other words, one of you is going to betray me. One of you is going to undermine me. One of you is going to discuss me with my enemies. One of you is going to hurt me. One of you is going to be ungrateful. One of you is going to forget all I have done for you. One of you is going to fight me from within. One of you is going to sell me to my enemies for a little bit of money.

Disloyalty has a way of cancelling out all your hard work. There are people who built churches and had them destroyed by one disloyal and treacherous associate.

## 7.    The symptom of worthlessness.

**Satan is called Belial, which means "useless". Watch out for THE SYMPTOM OF WORTHLESSNESS.** When the spirit of Belial visits you, all your efforts in the ministry will be made worthless. Anything, which nullifies and degrades your efforts is demonic. Anything that makes you into nothing, of no significance, of no value and makes you worthless is demonic. Belial is the spirit of worthlessness. Anything that trivialises your great ministry and your great input is the spirit of Belial. Persistent attempt to neutralise, nullify and trivialise your existence and importance is demonic.

When a community gives itself to drugs, crime, alcoholism, prostitution and other such activities, there is usually a lot of demonic presence. These activities degrade human beings and make them worthless. Whatever makes you worthless is of the devil! Do you know groups of people who are given to poverty, drugs, crime and alcoholism? There is often a high presence of evil spirits in such communities. Evil spirits seek to degrade human beings and make them worthless.

"And what concord hath Christ with Belial?..." (2 Corinthians 6:15). Where there are persistent and unusual occurrences that make your life worthless, you must think of the devil. Wherever there are activities that reduce a community to a low and worthless society, you must watch out for demon activity.

## 8.    The symptom of strife, quarrelling and war.

**And when the thousand years are expired, Satan shall be loosed out of his prison, And shall go out to deceive the nations which are in the four quarters of the earth, Gog and Magog, to GATHER THEM TOGETHER TO BATTLE: the number of whom is as the sand of the sea.**

**Revelation 20:7-8**

As you can see from this scripture, as soon as satan is loosed, he goes out to gather people to fight. Satan's work is to gather human beings and organise them to fight. Strife and confusion are symptoms of demonic presence. Wherever there is demonic activity there are quarrels, misunderstandings, confusion and every evil work.

**For where envying and strife is, there is confusion and every evil work.**

**James 3:16**

You must respect the reality that demons foster strife, quarrels and misunderstandings. This realization will keep you as far away from strife as possible. This realization will make you do all you can to avoid conflict and unnecessary strife. The strife that you find in churches and in marriages are some of the most certain signs of demon presence.

9.   **The symptom of unnatural things. You can detect demon activity by noticing how unnatural it is.**

**When He got out of the boat, immediately a man from the tombs with an unclean spirit met Him, and he had his dwelling among the tombs. And no one was able to bind him anymore, even with a chain; because he had often been bound with shackles and chains, and the chains had been torn apart by him and the shackles broken in pieces, and no one was strong enough to subdue him.**

**Constantly, night and day, he was screaming among the tombs and in the mountains, and gashing himself with stones.**

**Mark 5:2-5 (NASB)**

The story of this mad man with the unclean spirit shows that many unusual, illogical and persistent occurrences are demonic in nature. Unusual occurrences often reveal the presence of devils. There is a way things are expected to work out.

We all expect a certain behaviour and reaction from a normal human being. When you see unusual behaviour that makes no sense, you must think of demonic activity. For instance, the madman of Gadara lived in a cemetery. "...had his dwelling among the tombs..." (Mark 5:3). A normal person will not live in the mountains and among the dead. This unusual desire to live in a cemetery reveals the presence of devils.

The madman of Gadara who was also filled with thousands of demons cut himself with stones. "And always, night and day, he was in the mountains, and in the tombs, crying, and cutting himself with stones" (Mark 5:5). A normal person does not cut himself with stones because it is painful. It is very unusual for a person to cut himself with stones. When you notice unusual things that are destructive and negative, there is often an evil spirit behind them.

**10.  The symptom of persistence. You can detect demon activity by the persistence of a problem.**

Watch out for patterns of persistence!  The persistence and long continuance of unusual evils is a sign of demonic activity. Job experienced persistent attacks on his family, his life and his health. These incidents occurred one after the other and it looked as though Job was a man of great and persistent misfortune. We all know that the events that unfolded in Job's life were as a result of satan's direct attack on Job. "And the Lord said unto Satan, Behold, all that he hath is in thy power; only upon himself put not forth thine hand. So Satan went forth from the presence of the Lord" (Job 1:12).

Demons are relentless and persistent!  They are full time destroyers, tempters and accusers.  Relentless evil spirits leave a pattern of continuous and persistent harassment, intimidation, temptation and difficulty.  If you are beleaguered with persistent problems of long continuance, which have no solution, it must occur to you that there is a devil somewhere.

# CHAPTER 6

# How to Diagnose
# Demonic Activity

1.  You can diagnose demon activity by visions and
    revelations.

    And he shewed me Joshua the high priest standing
    before the angel of the Lord, and Satan standing at
    his right hand to resist him.

    And the Lord said unto Satan, The Lord rebuke
    thee, O Satan; even the Lord that hath chosen
    Jerusalem rebuke thee: is not this a brand plucked
    out of the fire?

    Now Joshua was clothed with filthy garments, and
    stood before the angel.

    And he answered and spake unto those that stood
    before him, saying, Take away the filthy garments
    from him. And unto him he said, Behold, I have
    caused thine iniquity to pass from thee, and I will
    clothe thee with change of raiment.

    **Zechariah 3:1-4**

There are times that God grants you divine revelations of the devil. Through visions and dreams, God may show you exactly what the devil is doing. Such revelations help you to focus on the real problem you are dealing with.

A man had a powerful vision in which he saw an evil spirit working in the life of a pastor's wife. In the vision, this evil spirit caused the couple to divorce. The evil spirit also caused the pastor's wife to be unfaithful to her husband. The pastor went through many problems in his life and ministry because his marriage broke down. In the vision, all the harassment and intimidation of the pastor was caused by evil spirits!

Through that vision, he was able to deal with the root cause of his marital problem. Thank God for visions and revelations that reveal demonic activity!

2.    **You can diagnose demon activity by a personal conviction.**

**But he turned, and said unto Peter, Get thee behind me, Satan: thou art an offence unto me: for thou savourest not the things that be of God, but those that be of men.**

**Matthew 16:23**

Jesus turned to Peter and knew that satan was speaking through him. Jesus did not see a vision. He had a strong conviction that satan was using his favourite disciple.

There are times when God will give you a conviction about the activity of devils. Such convictions are often difficult to prove. But you will have to walk by faith in your conviction that God has given you about an evil spirit. Always remember that a conviction can be as powerful as a vision. I came into the ministry based on a conviction and not a vision.

We walk by faith not by sight! You must believe in the things God shows you. There was a time that I developed a conviction about seven evil spirits that were following me. I knew, by conviction, exactly what the evil spirits were trying to do to me. I developed a strong conviction about the presence and manoeuvring of these creatures in my life. I decided to give them names so that I would remember them and bind them regularly. This helped me to develop defences against a persistent set of specific attacks against my life and ministry.

What is following you around? What is harassing you? What persistent struggles are you engaged in? Perhaps the Holy Spirit is revealing the identities of the evil spirits that are behind your struggle so that you deal with them effectively.

**3.    You can diagnose demon activity by hearing the devil speak through someone.**

**But he turned, and said unto Peter, Get thee behind me, Satan: thou art an offence unto me: for thou savourest not the things that be of God, but those that be of men.**

**Matthew 16:23**

It was Peter's voice but it was satan's words. It was Peter speaking but Jesus knew it was no other than satan. Every time someone speaks, it is possible that a spirit spoke through the person. When Jesus heard Peter speaking against the cross, He knew that satan was speaking through him. Today, there are few people who have a strong enough discernment to know that satan is speaking through someone. I once spoke to a pastor who confessed that his greatest mistake was to fail to diagnose the spirit of Jezebel in his senior pastor's wife. He told me that that mistake had cost him his job, his position, his income, his life and his ministry.

If you are filled with true discernment of the Holy Spirit, you will know when a spirit is speaking.

Do you remember how Jesus encouraged His disciples about not being afraid of knowing what to say? He told them, "It will not be you speaking, but the Spirit of the Father will speak through you." In other words, without a person knowing, a spirit can speak through you.

**For it is not ye that speak, but THE SPIRIT OF YOUR FATHER WHICH SPEAKETH in you.**

**Matthew 10:20**

I recently heard someone speaking and knew that satan was speaking through the person. I have heard satan speaking through a number of people. Sometimes, I could hear the voice of the accuser, the voice of the murderer and the voice of hatred. You will hear this voice when you know it. One day, as I listened to the voice of a young man, I instantly recognized the voice of satan. It's not really the content of what the person says. You can just tell that another person is speaking!

# CHAPTER 7

# Demons and the Impartation of Thoughts

(For the weapons of our warfare are not carnal, but mighty through God to the pulling down of strong holds;) CASTING DOWN IMAGINATIONS, and every high thing that exalteth itself against the knowledge of God, and bringing into captivity every thought to the obedience of Christ;

2 Corinthians 10:4-5

**D**emons are constantly imparting thoughts into people's minds. Your contact with a bad thought is your contact with an evil spirit. Thoughts show a spirit's presence. Demons constantly impart thoughts to your mind.

The worst spiritual attack you may ever experience may be a thought in your mind.

The most spiritual impartation you may ever receive can be thoughts in your mind.

The greatest sign you may ever have that a demon is nearby may be a negative thought or an idea. Negative thoughts are your contact with negative spirits!

## The Holy Spirit and the Impartation of Thoughts

Positive thoughts are your contact with positive spirits!

The greatest sign you may ever have that the Holy Spirit is nearby may be a thought or an idea.

When Jesus promised us the Holy Spirit, most people thought He would make everyone fall down and hear the sound of a rushing wind. The falling down and the sound of the rushing wind is what happened in the beginning when the Holy Spirit first arrived. But Jesus told us that the Holy Spirit would impart thoughts to our mind.

> **But the Comforter, which is the Holy Ghost, whom the Father will send in my name, he shall teach you all things, and BRING ALL THINGS TO YOUR REMEMBRANCE, (HYPOMIMNESKO) whatsoever I have said unto you.**
>
> **John 14:26**

Thoughts are symptoms and signs of the presence of a spirit. It is like seeing the droppings of a rat in your room. You do not need to see the rat to know that it is there. The pellets you see on the floor are the sign that it is there.

Thoughts that are revelations, indicate the presence of the Holy Spirit. Read the verse: "But the Comforter, which is the Holy Ghost, whom the Father will send in my name, he shall teach you all things, and bring all things to your remembrance (hypomimnesko), whatsoever I have said unto you" (John 14:26).

## *Hypomimnesko*: **The Impartation of Thoughts**

**But the Comforter, which is the Holy Ghost, whom the Father will send in my name, he shall teach you all things, and BRING ALL THINGS TO YOUR REMEMBRANCE (HYPOMIMNESKO), whatsoever I have said unto you.**

**John 14:26**

"*HYPOMIMNESKO*" means the impartation of thoughts.

"*HYPOMIMNESKO*" means to put something into your mind.

"*HYPOMIMNESKO*" is to put something into your remembrance.

"*HYPOMIMNESKO*" is to remind someone.

The depositing of something into your mind can be done by any kind of spirit. Therefore one of the most spiritual experiences you may ever have is to have certain thoughts put into your mind. Likewise the impartation of something into your mind can be done by any kind of spirit. Therefore the closest contact you may ever have with a spirit is to have certain thoughts put into your mind. The impartation of something in your mind can be done by the Holy Spirit.

The impartation of something in your mind is to experience *HYPOMIMNESKO*.

There are two types of *hypomimnesko*, or impartations of thoughts that come into everyone's minds. Some impartations of thoughts are direct, injected and easily noticed individual thoughts. Such direct, injected and imparted thoughts are dangerous but easily detected.

Some impartations of thoughts are indirect, unnoticed, pervading opinions and beliefs. These impartations of thoughts are very dangerous indeed!

Established thoughts and attitudes are indications of long-standing influences of spirits. Philosophers are a type of human being who inject and impart thoughts, ideas and attitudes into the world. Such people can release the most amazing widespread attitudes and opinions into the world.

Examples of famous impartation of thoughts and ideas are from people like Darwin and Robert Ingersoll. They can be blamed for the impartation of the widespread and pervading atheism and humanism in Europe. (Humanism is a line of thinking that emphasizes human reasoning, human fulfilment, human achievement, human science, but rejects the importance of belief in God).

The sweeping, dominating and pervading culture of disloyalty in a church shows you the presence of a mighty evil spirit that has imparted confusion, discontentment, treachery, murmuring and disloyalty into a church. Such attitudes are sown by certain people and can remain in the church for many years.

The sweeping, pervading culture of corruption and fornication in certain parts of the world are also evidence of a mighty evil spirit who dominates that section of the world. The culture of widespread acceptance of abominations in the world today shows the presence of evil spirits everywhere.

Some places have a pervading culture of rebellion against authority. They can insult any kind of leader, including their president and get away with it. In such places, the idea of being told what to do is out of the question. This pervading culture of rebellion and disrespect is evidence of a formidable evil spirit who has imparted certain thoughts and attitudes into the masses.

A pervading love for God, a pervading love for the work of God, a strong faith in Jesus Christ and the love for evangelism is a sign of the presence of the Holy Spirit. The Holy Spirit has imparted thoughts about the love of God into the church. You will notice that, years ago, there was a pervading culture of sacrificing your life for God. The absence of thoughts about the Cross and thoughts about laying down your life for Jesus shows the absence of the Holy Spirit.

## Men Can Impart Thoughts into You

The impartation of thoughts into your mind can be done by men:

And he said unto them, TAKE HEED WHAT YE HEAR: with what measure ye mete, it shall be measured to you: and unto you that hear shall more be given.

Mark 4:24

## The Holy Spirit Can Impart Thoughts into You

The impartation of thoughts into your mind can be done by the Holy Spirit:

But the Comforter, which is the Holy Ghost, whom the Father will send in my name, he shall teach you all things, and BRING ALL THINGS TO YOUR REMEMBRANCE, whatsoever I have said unto you.

John 14: 26

## Angels Can Impart Thoughts into You

The impartation of thoughts into your mind can be done by angels - revelation can be imparted by angels:

The Revelation of Jesus Christ, which God gave unto him, to shew unto his servants things which must shortly come to pass; and he sent and signified it BY HIS ANGEL unto his servant John:

Revelations 1:1

## Demons Can Impart Thoughts into You

The impartation of thoughts into your mind can be done by demons:

CASTING DOWN IMAGINATIONS, and every high thing that exalteth itself against the knowledge of God, and bringing into captivity every thought to the obedience of Christ;

2 Corinthians 10:5

# CHAPTER 8

# Demonic Operations and Manoeuvres

A ll through the Bible, you see different types of demonic manoeuvres and operations. A demonic operation is a move made by the devil against you. Satan seeks to do different things to different people. Sometimes, he oppresses. At other times, he possesses! To possess someone is to own the person totally. Sometimes, devils do not own people, but they seduce them to do evil.

At other times demons enter a person and mix with the human being, producing a demon-infiltrated human being. Such demon-human hybrids are the result of demonic infiltration of the human race by evil spirits.

Indeed, there are times that good people are divinely exposed to continual demonic harassment. This continual demonic harassment is called "demonic buffeting".

## 1.    DEMONIC OPPRESSION

How God anointed Jesus of Nazareth with the Holy Ghost and with power: who went about doing good, and HEALING ALL THAT WERE OPPRESSED of the devil; for God was with him.

Acts 10:38

Demonic oppression is sickness and disease! Virtually all diseases are a result of demonic oppression. To oppress someone is to harshly control a person. Demonic oppression is the harsh control of human beings with demonic burdens and cruel impositions. Demonic oppression is when a person is weighed down and burdened by disease.

## 2. DEMONIC POSSESSION

Demon possession is when demons have full control of a person. It is not possible to control a nation, a person or an organisation, until you have control of the head. It is when demons control the head, the brain or the mind of a person that it is termed demonic possession.

When demons control a person totally, they own him and do to him whatever they please. People who are possessed by the devil experience specific symptoms which medical doctors call schizophrenia. When a person is completely mad, he is possessed by demons. These demons speak to the mad man, accuse him, insult him and direct him. Mad people take off their clothes, lose contact with reality, become violent and virtually turn into animals. In a mad person you can see what the devil would like to do to you if he had the chance. You must do whatever you have to, to prevent demons entering you. Anytime demons live in a person they desire to possess him completely and take over.

And they come to Jesus, and see him that was possessed with the devil, and had the legion, sitting, and clothed, and in his right mind: and they were afraid.

And they that saw it told them how it befell TO HIM THAT WAS POSSESSED with the devil, and also concerning the swine.

Mark 5:15-16

## 3. DEMONIC SEDUCTION

Now the Spirit speaketh expressly, that in the latter times some shall depart from the faith, giving heed to SEDUCING SPIRITS, and doctrines of devils;

1 Timothy 4:1

Seduction is the act of being led astray by demons. Seduction is the process of deliberately enticing a person! To seduce somebody is to engage a person in a relationship and to lead a person astray. Seducing spirits keep you away from your duty and from what is right. A seducing spirit is sent to corrupt or to persuade you to engage in sexual immorality. The word "seduction" stems from Latin and means literally "to lead astray". The Bible speaks clearly about seducing spirits. These spirits have discussions with you and try to persuade you to believe in what is not true. There are several examples of people who were seduced, persuaded and eventually destroyed by demons. Eve was led astray because she was seduced by the devil. Ahab was led to his destruction by an evil spirit. Seduction is a very dangerous demonic manoeuvre because it involves your being led astray instead of being led by the Holy Spirit.

## 4.    DEMONIC TRANSIENT EMPLOYMENT

Demonic transient employment is when satan temporarily uses a person to speak to you. You need to know how to detect the voice of satan when he speaks through a human being. Jesus' most senior assistant, apostle Peter was transiently deployed to speak to Jesus Christ. Anyone who allows it can be used as a voice of satan. Both Timothy and Titus were warned about wives being transiently used as devils. When pastors' wives and older women are slanderers and false accusers they are transiently employed as devils.

> Then Peter took him, and began to rebuke him, saying, Be it far from thee, Lord: this shall not be unto thee. But he turned, and said unto Peter, Get thee behind me, Satan: thou art an offence unto me: for thou savourest not the things that be of God, but those that be of men.
>
> Matthew 16:22-23

> Even so must their wives be grave, not slanderers (DEVILS), sober, faithful in all things.
>
> 1 Timothy 3:11

The aged women likewise, that they be in behaviour as becometh holiness, not false accusers (DEVILS), not given to much wine, teachers of good things;

Titus 2:3

## 5. DEMONIC ENTRANCE

Demonic entrance is when the devil enters a person. Usually, this is after the devil has been seducing and harassing the individual for some time. A demonic entry is great penetration that has been sought by the demons for years. When satan enters into someone he is able to accomplish a greater evil by his presence within the person. When satan entered into Judas he accomplished the murder of Jesus Christ.

THEN ENTERED SATAN INTO JUDAS surnamed Iscariot, being of the number of the twelve. And he went his way, and communed with the chief priests and captains, how he might betray him unto them.

Luke 22:3-4

Then goeth he, and taketh with himself SEVEN OTHER SPIRITS more wicked than himself, and THEY ENTER IN and dwell there: and the last state of that man is worse than the first. Even so shall it be also unto this wicked generation.

Matthew 12:45

## 6. DEMONIC MIXING

Demonic mixing is the blending and uniting of evil spirits and men to produce parahumans and hybrids. The concept of a human being blending with a spirit to produce a hybrid is well accepted by the church. Remember that Jesus Christ was produced by the Holy Spirit coming upon the holy virgin Mary. Mary was a human being and the Holy Spirit is a spirit.

The long history of wickedness by human beings proves that mankind have mingled with evil spirits and produced much evil throughout the ages. The Bible has a simple passage that proves the fact that many human beings have blended with devils. The Book of Enoch also teaches these realities.

> That the sons of God saw the daughters of men that they were fair; and they TOOK THEM WIVES of all which they chose. And the Lord said, My spirit shall not always strive with man, for that he also is flesh: yet his days shall be an hundred and twenty years. There were giants in the earth in those days; and also after that, when the sons of God came in unto the daughters of men, and they bare children to them, the same became mighty men which were of old, men of renown.
>
> Genesis 6:2-4

## 7. DEMONIC BUFFETING

Demonic buffeting is when a demon is allowed to have access to a saint of God for a specific purpose. It is as though the demon is sent by God to torment His own children.

Job experienced this in a terrible way. Such buffeting can and does produce sickness, death, robbery and tragedy. God allowed satan to tempt Job but did not allow satan to kill him.

The apostle Paul also experienced the phenomenon of demonic buffeting. An evil spirit was allowed to buffet him in order to keep him humble.

## Paul and Demonic Buffeting

> And lest I should be exalted above measure through the abundance of the revelations, there was given to me a thorn in the flesh, THE MESSENGER OF SATAN TO BUFFET ME, lest I should be exalted above measure. For this thing I besought the Lord thrice, that it might depart from me. And he said unto me, My grace is sufficient for thee: for my strength is made perfect in weakness. Most

gladly therefore will I rather glory in my infirmities, that the power of Christ may rest upon me.

2 Corinthians 12:7-9

## Job and Demonic Buffeting

And the Lord said unto Satan, Hast thou considered my servant Job, that there is none like him in the earth, a perfect and an upright man, one that feareth God, and escheweth evil? And still he holdeth fast his integrity, although thou movedst me against him, to destroy him without cause. And Satan answered the Lord, and said, Skin for skin, yea, all that a man hath will he give for his life. But put forth thine hand now, and touch his bone and his flesh, and he will curse thee to thy face. And THE LORD SAID UNTO SATAN, BEHOLD, HE IS IN THINE HAND; BUT SAVE HIS LIFE. So went Satan forth from the presence of the Lord, and smote Job with sore boils from the sole of his foot unto his crown.

Job 2:3-7

# CHAPTER 9

# Demonic Seduction

Now the Spirit speaketh expressly, that in the latter times some shall depart from the faith, giving heed to SEDUCING SPIRITS, and doctrines of devils;

1 Timothy 4:1

**W**ith demonic discussions you are seduced to believe what is not true. It is a to and fro thought process with devils up, close and personal. The effect of having been seduced by a devil is amazing. Devils are out there waiting to seduce whoever is willing to talk. Eve was seduced and destroyed by satan. Ahab was seduced by an evil spirit and killed. Satan attempted to seduce Jesus Christ but failed. Satan will always try to seduce you and lead you astray from the will of God.

## Eve Was Seduced

And Adam was not deceived, but THE WOMAN BEING DECEIVED was in the transgression.

1 Timothy 2:14

Now the serpent was more subtil than any beast of the field which the Lord God had made. And he said unto the woman, Yea, hath God said, Ye shall not eat of every tree of the garden? And the woman said unto the serpent, We may eat of the fruit of the trees of the garden: But of the fruit of the tree which is in the midst of the garden, God hath said, Ye shall not eat of it, neither shall ye touch it, lest ye die. And the serpent said unto the woman, Ye shall not surely die:

Genesis 3:1-4

## Ahab was Seduced

And the Lord said, who shall persuade Ahab, that he may go up and fall at Ramoth-Gilead? And one said on this manner, and another said on that manner. And there came forth a spirit, and stood before the Lord, and said, I will persuade him.

1 Kings 22:20-21

And for this cause God shall send them STRONG DELUSION, THAT THEY SHOULD BELIEVE A LIE:

2 Thessalonians 2:11

## Satan Attempted to Seduce Jesus

Then was Jesus led up of the Spirit into the wilderness to be tempted of the devil. And when he had fasted forty days and forty nights, he was afterward an hungred.

And when the tempter came to him, he said, if thou be the Son of God, command that these stones be made bread. But he answered and said, it is written, Man shall not live by bread alone, but by every word that proceedeth out of the mouth of God.

Matthew 4:1-4

## Effects of Demonic Seduction

A short discussion with a demon leads to seduction. Evil spirits have a devastating and contaminating effect on people. The presence of an evil spirit radically changes a person. If you are trained, you can tell when people have interacted with the devil before. The best way to learn about the effect of demons on a person is to examine the impact that satan had on Adam and Eve.

The short conversation with satan, changed our great great grandfather and mother forever. The short interaction of Adam and Eve with satan changed the human race for ever. Any interaction you have with the devil will change your life drastically. Any interaction with the devil leads to an impartation of satanic nature and satanic characteristics. It seems that the nature of the human being itself is changed by interacting with satan. There seems to be a lingering effect of this interaction.

What were the devastating effects of satan's seduction of Adam and Eve?

## 1. Demonic seduction results in a compulsion to hide.

**And they heard the voice of the Lord God walking in the garden in the cool of the day: and ADAM AND HIS WIFE HID THEMSELVES FROM THE PRESENCE OF THE LORD God amongst the trees of the garden.**

**Genesis 3:8**

Adam and Eve's first reaction after interacting with the devil was to hide among the trees. Adam and Eve wanted to disappear into the vegetation. Adam and Eve wanted God to mistake them for one of the trees. They wanted to blend in and become unnoticeable.

Watch out for quiet people who say nothing and hide among the trees. They have been affected by something evil. Today, many people have a compulsion to hide. You will notice how some people want to sit at the back and never be seen in church.

"Were you in church?"

"Oh yes, I was there."

"But I didn't see you."

"Oh, I was there."

This is how the conversation usually goes with these mysterious members.

They want to stay in the shadows and come up with a greeting at the end of the programme. There are various reasons why people hide in the shadows. Staying away, hiding and secrecy are symptoms of demonic affectation.

On the other hand, when people are affected by the Holy Spirit, they want to sit in front. They smile at you happily, cheerfully and knowingly. When people are filled with the Holy Spirit, they talk to you and relate to you happily.

Watch out for people who claim that their culture does not allow them to chat freely and relate normally.

Your compulsion to hide must be replaced with the compulsion to be open. Decide to be yourself; to be open, to be bare and to be known. This shows that satan has not contaminated, corrupted and destroyed something in your life.

## 2. Demonic seduction results in fears.

**And the Lord God called unto Adam, and said unto him, where art thou? And he said, I HEARD THY VOICE IN THE GARDEN, AND I WAS AFRAiD, because I was naked; and I hid myself.**

**Genesis 3:9-10**

Watch out for those who are afraid of everything! Fear is a spirit! Fear is not a mood, an attitude or a feeling! Fear is an evil spirit! People who are affected by the devil have all sorts of fears. The fear of the unknown! The fear of tomorrow! The fear of men! The fear of women! The fear of death! The fear of poverty!

These are just a few of the many fears that affect your life. Remember that when you were a little child, you had no fears! As you grew up in this world and interacted with the devil, you developed many different fears. Fear is an evil spirit! Fear is not an attitude or a mood. David prayed to be delivered from his fears because fears are destructive.

**I sought the LORD, and he heard me, and delivered me from all my fears.**

**Psalms 34:4**

People who are led by the fear of poverty will do many illegal things in order to have money. Many women marry out of the fear of never getting married. Such a marriage has an evil spirit in its foundation. You should marry out of love! Perfect love casts out fear and fear is a very poor substitute for love.

## 3. Demonic seduction results in you being over-conscious of certain things.

**And he said, WHO TOLD THEE THAT THOU WAST NAKED? Hast thou eaten of the tree, whereof I commanded thee that thou shouldest not eat?**

**Genesis 3:11**

Adam and Eve became conscious of the fact that they were naked. Nakedness was something that had been with them all along.

Their private parts and genitals had been swinging around freely for years. Suddenly, after their interaction with the devil, they became conscious of these genital organs. This consciousness of certain things is one of the tell-tale signs of interaction with an evil spirit. Today, we are conscious of many things that reveal that we have interacted with and have been influenced by devils.

In some parts of the world, people are very conscious of colour. Are you a white man, a black man, a yellow man or a green man? Some people are so conscious of colour that they have nothing to do with people of another colour. It is the consciousness of colour that has led to many of the evils of our world today. There are people who would not read my book if they saw my colour. Such colour consciousness is truly demonic.

We once had a crusade in a country where there are both white and black people. The white pastor who was approached to participate in our crusade smiled at the crusade director and said, "I admire your boldness in inviting us. But I have to tell you that our white congregations will not participate in your crusade because it is being organised by black people."

Wow, what a shock! I later saw a great participation of these white congregations and pastors in a similar crusade that was being organised by a white man from America.

In many countries, no one was very conscious of the different tribes that existed. However, after a series of elections, a great consciousness and awareness of which tribe a person belonged to, began to arise. This consciousness of which tribe you come from reveals the presence of devils. Democratic elections which stir up tribal sentiments reveal the impact of demons.

When I was growing up in secondary school, my best friends were from a certain tribe. I was never conscious of their tribe. However, after an election, I looked back and realised that many of my friends came from a certain tribe. I had never been conscious of anyone's tribe before that.

This is the question the Lord God asked Adam and Eve. "Who told you that you were naked?" Who made you conscious of your nakedness? Who told you that you were a white man? When did you become conscious of the fact that you are a white man? Who told you that you are a black man? Who told you that you were from this tribe? Who made you conscious of tribes in your country?

In Rwanda, people became very conscious of whether they were Hutus or Tutsis. It is satan who makes people over-conscious of certain aspects of God's creation.

The consciousness of the differences between Hutus and Tutsis in Rwanda led them to the famous genocide that killed a million people.

Some pastors are extra conscious of the rich and the famous. The question the Lord God could ask at this time is, "Why are you conscious of riches, power and money?" Your interaction with satan has made you conscious of things you should not be conscious of.

Human beings' consciousness of their reproductive organs and their naturally created differences have led to a heightened awareness of sex and a great increase in sexual sin and perversions. None of the innocent animals of the forest hide their genitals like we do. None of them have sex secretly like we do and none of them create the evil that we do. This is because animals have not been affected by satan and sin in the way we have been.

Examine your life. What are you extra-conscious of? What demonic interaction has made you so conscious of colour, tribe, money and sex in the wrong way?

# CHAPTER 10

# Demonic Entry: Why Demons Want to Enter You

When the unclean spirit is gone out of a man, he walketh through dry places, seeking rest, and findeth none. Then he saith, I WILL RETURN INTO MY HOUSE from whence I came out; and when he is come, he findeth it empty, swept, and garnished.

**Matthew 12:43-44**

# Evidence that Demons Have Entered Human Beings

Three are demons in the most ordinary-looking people around you. In my ministry I have encountered many ordinary people who were possessed and influenced by devils.

Here are four pieces of evidence that evil spirits have entered and infiltrated human beings.

1.  **The behaviour of the human race is the greatest evidence of the infiltration of evil spirits.** The sin and wickedness in our world matches the wickedness that was in the days of Noah. Solomon knew this reality and said "…also the heart of the sons of men is full of evil, and madness is in their heart while they live, and after that they go to the dead" (Ecclesiastes 9:3). The apostle, John said, the whole world lies in wickedness. "And we know that we are of God, and the whole world lieth in wickedness." (1 John 5:19).

2.  **Jesus Christ was preaching in the synagogue and one of the worshippers was found to have a demon within.** This demon had been hiding securely in this worshipper for many years but was forced out because of the presence of Jesus Christ. "And there was in their synagogue a man with an unclean spirit; and he cried out, Saying, Let us alone; what have we to do with thee, thou Jesus of Nazareth? Art thou come to destroy us? I know thee who thou art, the Holy One of God. And Jesus rebuked him, saying, Hold thy peace, and come out of him." (Mark 1:23-25)

3.  **Jesus cast out as many as six thousand demons from one man.** A legion is about six thousand men. So the mad man of Gadara had about six thousand demons in him. "For he said unto him, Come out of the man, thou

unclean spirit. And he asked him, What is thy name? And he answered, saying, My name is Legion: for we are many" (Mark 5:8-9).

4. Paul encountered demons that were living in people and even prophesying truths. "It happened that as we were going to the place of prayer, a slave-girl having a spirit of divination met us, who was bringing her masters much profit by fortune-telling. Following after Paul and us, she kept crying out, saying, "These men are bond-servants of the Most High God, who are proclaiming to you the way of salvation." She continued doing this for many days. But Paul was greatly annoyed, and turned and said to the spirit, "I command you in the name of Jesus Christ to come out of her!" And it came out at that very moment." (Acts 16:16-18, NASB)

## Why Demons Want to Enter Human Beings

1. **Demons want to enter people because when they are outside the human body they get thirsty.**

**When the unclean spirit is gone out of a man, he walketh through DRY PLACES, seeking rest, and findeth none.**
**Matthew 12:43**

The human body provides nourishment to demons. Their thirst and desires are fulfilled by drinking from a human being or animal. Everywhere outside the human being is considered as a dry place.

You must remember that demons are often compared to insects and flies. Most insects drink something from the human being. The anopheles mosquito, for instance, drinks blood from a human being.

When these insects drink and eat off the human body they cause disease to come to the body. The body begins to malfunction and temperatures go up. Insects drink and feed off the human being and cause untold discomfort and disease.

When evil spirits drink the flesh and the blood of human beings to quench their thirst, they cause all sorts of problems, diseases and depravities to occur in the human being. I remember the testimony of a lady who was dying of lung cancer. She had a few more days to live. She was basically a bag of skin and bones and the doctors had given up on her. On the fifth day of the miracle service, the pastor had a vision when he laid his hands on her. He saw a little imp-like creature hanging onto her chest. Apparently, this creature was sucking her life away, just like an insect would. When the pastor commanded this creature to leave the lady's body, it jumped down onto the ground and began to walk out of the church. Can you believe that this lady who was left with a few more days to live, suddenly began to recover, gained back weight and was completely healed of the cancer.

Once you picture evil spirits as insect-like creatures, which suck life and cause fever, weight loss, malaise and general illness, you will begin to understand what you are dealing with in evil spirits.

## 2. Demons want to enter you because when they are outside the human body they have no rest.

A human being provides great comfort and rest to demons. A person rests in his comfort zone where he is in the midst of familiar things. Demons are so attracted to human beings because in the human being they find familiar things which set them at ease.

Once they are in a body they have the mind, the speech organs, the sex organs, the emotions, the desires, the feelings and the personalities which they are so used to. Having inhabited several different people, they are most at home with human organs and the human body.

**When the unclean spirit is gone out of a man, he walketh through dry places, SEEKING REST, and findeth none.**

**Matthew 12:43**

You must notice how the presence of demons causes people to have abnormal personalities, abnormal behaviour, abnormal responses, abnormal sex, abnormal desires and abnormal feelings.

You must also realise how the presence of demons causes people to have illnesses like cancers, swellings and inflammations of different parts of their bodies.

It is also the presence of evil spirits that causes men to lack compassion and become murderers, killers and thieves. The personalities of ordinary men are completely distorted as they become murderers, wounding and killing at random.

The abnormal sexual desires of both girls and boys can also be attributed to demons who are very comfortable stimulating these body parts. Demons cause the increased desire of human beings for sex by taking their rest in the sexual parts of the human body. They also cause a desire for abnormal sex of men between men and women between women. You will notice that as demonic infiltration and evil has increased in our world, the most unusual perversions, including having sex with animals, are on the increase. All these abnormal desires and abnormal feelings are caused by demons who feed on these organs, they stimulate them and make them abnormal.

## 3.    Demons want to enter you because they see you as a house.

Evil spirits see you as a home. Many insects and living creatures live inside the human being. In the study of microbiology, the creatures that live inside the human body see the human body as a home or a host. Many insects live in animals and consider these as their permanent homes. Dogs are hosts and homes to the *leishmania infantum* which causes *leishmaniasis*. Pigs are hosts for *cestode worms*. Snails are hosts for *schistosomiasis*. Fowls are hosts for *avian influenza*. As you can see, several of these disease-causing creatures see other animals as their homes.

**Then he saith, I will return INTO MY HOUSE from whence I came out; and when he is come, he findeth it empty, swept, and garnished.**

**Matthew 12:44**

Several parasites, bacteria and even viruses live in human beings and consider the human body as their home. Every time you pass by, evil spirits look at you longingly and say to themselves, "I wish I could live there. I wish that was my home." Just as human beings pass by and look longingly at mansions in an affluent neighbourhood, demons look at you and desire to live in you one day.

It is important that you deny evil spirits the opportunity to live in you. As you read on, you will see how to prevent evil spirits from moving in to live in you. Demons are so desirous to have a home that they would rather go into pigs than to be without a body. They pleaded with Jesus to be allowed to enter the pigs. They preferred to live in these pigs than to live on trees and in the open. It is because many animals are filled with evil spirits that you must pray before you eat meat. When people eat rotten meat and have food poisoning, it is because living creatures called bacteria come to live in your body.

4.    **Demons want to enter you because in you they can have fellowship with fellow demons and form a demon gang.**

Demons see you as a centre for good demon fellowship. Demon gangs live together in human beings. They are most comfortable with fellow demon creatures. Jesus told us that one evil spirit fetched seven more wicked spirits and they all took up residence in the same man.

**Then goeth he, and TAKETH WITH HIMSELF SEVEN OTHER SPIRITS more wicked than himself, and they enter in and dwell there: and the last state of that man is worse than the first. Even so shall it be also unto this wicked generation.**

**Matthew 12:45**

The more demons that are in one man, the more problems and the more difficult it is for that individual. Jesus said that the state of that man was worse because he had seven more demons in him. To have a legion of demons is to have an uncountable number of evil spirits in you. This is what leads to what we call "full possession" by the devil. A fully possessed person has almost every part of his being occupied by one or other evil spirit and there is very little space for normalcy.

The demons prefer to live in groups or gangs, otherwise the evil spirit would have come back to live in the house and selfishly closed the door to other spirits. But this is not what happened. The demon was happy to get seven other demons to make the home warmer and livelier.

This is why most evil spirits develop into teams or gangs.

# CHAPTER 11

# Demonic Oppression:
# What Is It?

How God anointed Jesus of Nazareth with the Holy
Ghost and with power: who went about doing good,
and HEALING ALL THAT WERE OPPRESSED
of the devil; for God was with him.

Acts 10:38

**D**emonic oppression is the cause of many illnesses and diseases. You must know about evil spirits because they cause diseases. *Diseases are caused by demonic oppression.* Modern science has shown us many of the invisible physical causes of diseases. There are bacteria, viruses and parasites that cause many illnesses. Unless you believe in science, you will not believe in the existence of bacteria, viruses or parasites. The reason why the Ebola virus spread easily in Africa is because many of the people did not believe in the scientific causes of the disease. People would handle the dead bodies of the Ebola victims and get the disease.

Similarly, unless you are a spiritual person, you will not believe or accept that many illnesses are actually caused by the oppression of evil spirits. You see, behind these bacteria, viruses and parasites are evil spirits.

Today, there are groups of people who do not believe in either science or in the spiritual world. Both of these groups are making a mistake. Bacteria, parasites, viruses, demons and fallen angels are very real! For many years, before the invention of microscopes, human beings did not know about the existence of bacteria and parasites. Today, with the invention of these magnifying glasses and lenses, we are able to see parasites and bacteria. Maybe one day there will be an invention that will open up the spirit world where demons and other creatures will be seen clearly. Human beings will be extremely surprised to see the real cause of many problems.

Jesus cast out demons from people when he healed them. He knew demons were oppressing people and causing diseases like deafness and dumbness and so He cast out those evil spirits. If you are to be Christ-like, you must follow the example of Jesus. In your ministry, you will need to cast out devils if you are to see the healing and miracle anointing at work. The fact that you know some medical facts does not rule out the reality of demonic oppression in our world today. I want to show you several examples of how demons caused diseases in the time of Jesus.

Each one of these cases is an example of demonic oppression causing illness.

## 1.  Oppression of the devil causes epilepsy.

And one of the multitude answered and said, Master, I have brought unto thee my son, which hath a dumb spirit; And wheresoever he taketh him, he teareth him: and he foameth, and gnasheth with his teeth, and pineth away: and I spake to thy disciples that they should cast him out; and they could not.

He answereth him, and saith, O faithless generation, how long shall I be with you? How long shall I suffer you? Bring him unto me. And they brought him unto him: and when he saw him, straightway the spirit tare him; and he fell on the ground, and wallowed foaming. And he asked his father, how long is it ago since this came unto him? And he said, of a child. And ofttimes it hath cast him into the fire, and into the waters, to destroy him: but if thou canst do any thing, have compassion on us, and help us.

Jesus said unto him, If thou canst believe, all things are possible to him that believeth. And straightway the father of the child cried out, and said with tears, Lord, I believe; help thou mine unbelief. When Jesus saw that the people came running together, HE REBUKED THE FOUL SPIRIT, saying unto him, Thou dumb and deaf spirit, I charge thee, come out of him, and enter no more into him. And the spirit cried, and rent him sore, and came out of him: and he was as one dead; insomuch that many said, He is dead.

Mark 9:17-26

## 2.  Oppression of the devil causes diseases of bones and joints.

And he was teaching in one of the synagogues on the sabbath.

And, behold, there was a woman which had a SPIRIT OF INFIRMITY eighteen years, and WAS BOWED

TOGETHER, AND COULD IN NO WISE LIFT UP HERSELF. And when Jesus saw her, he called her to him, and said unto her, Woman, thou art loosed from thine infirmity. And he laid his hands on her: and immediately she was made straight, and glorified God. . . .

The Lord then answered him, and said, Thou hypocrite, doth not each one of you on the sabbath loose his ox or his ass from the stall, and lead him away to watering? And ought not this woman, being a daughter of Abraham, WHOM SATAN HATH BOUND, lo, these eighteen years, be loosed from this bond on the sabbath day?

Luke 13:10-13, 15-16

### 3.  Oppression of the devil causes deafness and dumbness.

When Jesus saw that the people came running together, he rebuked the foul spirit, saying unto him, Thou DUMB AND DEAF SPIRIT, I charge thee, come out of him, and enter no more into him.

Mark 9:25

### 4.  Oppression of the devil causes blindness.

Then was brought unto him one possessed WITH A DEVIL, BLIND, and dumb: and he healed him, insomuch that the blind and dumb both spake and saw. And all the people were amazed, and said, Is not this the son of David?

Matthew 12:22-23

Even good angels were able to strike people with blindness. This shows how spiritual, blindness is.

But the men put forth their hand, and pulled Lot into the house to them, and shut to the door. And they SMOTE THE MEN that were at the door of the house WITH BLINDNESS, both small and great: so that they wearied themselves to find the door.

Genesis 19:10-11

## 5. Oppression of the devil causes many illnesses in the multitudes.

When the even was come, they brought unto him MANY THAT WERE POSSESSED WITH DEVILS: AND HE CAST OUT THE SPIRITS WITH HIS WORD, AND HEALED ALL THAT WERE SICK: That it might be fulfilled which was spoken by Esaias the prophet, saying, Himself took our infirmities, and bare our sicknesses.

Matthew 8:16-17

Now when the sun was setting, all they that had any sick with divers diseases brought them unto him; and HE LAID HIS HANDS ON EVERY ONE OF THEM, AND HEALED THEM. AND DEVILS ALSO CAME OUT OF MANY, crying out, and saying, Thou art Christ the Son of God. And he rebuking them suffered them not to speak: for they knew that he was Christ.

Luke 4:40-41

And all the city was gathered together at the door. And HE HEALED MANY THAT WERE SICK OF DIVERS DISEASES, AND CAST OUT MANY DEVILS; and suffered not the devils to speak, because they knew him.

Mark 1:33-34

# CHAPTER 12

# Demonic Oppression: How You Can Be Free From It

You can be set free from demon power through the ministry of Jesus Christ. Jesus Christ demonstrated the various methods of getting free from demonic oppression. In your ministry today, you can employ all these methods to set people free from demonic oppression.

1. **You can be set free from demon power through the anointing of the Holy Spirit.**

And it shall come to pass in that day, that his burden shall be taken away from off thy shoulder, and his yoke from off thy neck, and THE YOKE SHALL BE DESTROYED BECAUSE OF THE ANOINTING.

Isaiah 10:27

How GOD ANOINTED JESUS of Nazareth with the Holy Ghost and with power: who went about doing good, and healing all that were oppressed of the devil; for God was with him.

Acts 10:38

It is the anointing that breaks the yoke. The anointing of the Holy Spirit is the power of the Holy Spirit that works behind the scenes to ensure that the word of God is established. Without the power of God, you and I are nothing but ordinary human beings, ordinary sinners and ordinary failures. The power of God in action in your life is the anointing of the Holy Spirit. Even Jesus Christ needed to be anointed with power and the Holy Spirit in order to do the work of God.

Jesus was anointed to heal and therefore you will need to be anointed to heal too. Without the anointing, Jesus would have remained a carpenter. Without the anointing, Jesus would have continued building wardrobes, doors and furniture. Without the anointing Jesus would have continued making coffins, repairing roofs and fixing wooden structures. That is exactly what every ordinary carpenter did.

However, when Jesus was anointed, He was transformed into another man. He became the Anointed Saviour that we know so well. As you can see, the anointing is the secret behind the miracles! The anointing is the secret behind the success! The anointing is the secret behind the power! It is the anointing that breaks the yoke!

2.    **You can be set free from demon power through the spoken Word.**

When the even was come, they brought unto him many that were possessed with devils: and HE CAST OUT THE SPIRITS WITH HIS WORD, and healed all that were sick:

Matthew 8:16

3.    **You can be set free from demon power through the laying on of hands.**

And he was teaching in one of the synagogues on the sabbath.

And, behold, there was a woman which had a spirit of infirmity eighteen years, and was bowed together, and could in no wise lift up herself. And when Jesus saw her, he called her to him, and said unto her, Woman, thou art loosed from thine infirmity. And HE LAID HIS HANDS ON HER: AND IMMEDIATELY SHE WAS MADE STRAIGHT, and glorified God.

The Lord then answered him, and said, Thou hypocrite, doth not each one of you on the sabbath loose his ox or his ass from the stall, and lead him away to watering? And ought not this woman, being a daughter of Abraham, whom satan hath bound, lo, these eighteen years, be loosed from this bond on the sabbath day?

Luke 13:10-13, 15-16

This case illustrates the wickedness of devils. Jesus Christ told us clearly that this woman had a spirit of infirmity. This evil spirit caused the woman to bend over and remain in that position for eighteen years. Although there have been many wicked tyrants in the world, few would have been known to inflict such inhuman suffering for so long.

In boarding schools all over the world, tyrannical seniors inflict terrible punishment on their juniors. None of these wicked seniors would ever inflict a spine-twisting punishment for eighteen long years.

Eighteen years is a long time to twist a person's back. This particular healing reveals not only the compassion of Jesus Christ but also the wickedness of evil spirits.

### 4. You can be set free from demon power by rebuking the devil.

And when they were come to the multitude, there came to him a certain man, kneeling down to him, and saying, Lord, have mercy on my son: for he is lunatick, and sore vexed: for ofttimes he falleth into the fire, and oft into the water. And I brought him to thy disciples, and they could not cure him. Then Jesus answered and said, O faithless and perverse generation, how long shall I be with you? How long shall I suffer you? Bring him hither to me. And JESUS REBUKED THE DEVIL; AND HE DEPARTED

OUT OF HIM: and the child was cured from that very hour.

Matthew 17:14-18

Satan hears the words that you speak. When you rebuke him, he is rebuked! When you sack him, he is sacked! When you banish him he is banished! When you bind him, he is bound! When you block him, he is blocked! It is important to speak the word of God against the devil. It is important to release the harshest rebukes against evil spirits. Drive them out of your presence. Declare judgments against them. Fight and contend against them in the spirit. Use words of faith and pronounce great declarations of fiery judgment against all creatures in the invisible world that surround your dwelling place.

**5.   You can be set free from demon power through your lifestyle of fasting and prayer.**

Then came the disciples to Jesus apart, and said, why could not we cast him out? And Jesus said unto them, Because of your unbelief: for verily I say unto you, If ye have faith as a grain of mustard seed, ye shall say unto this mountain, Remove hence to yonder place; and it shall remove; and nothing shall be impossible unto you. Howbeit THIS KIND GOETH NOT OUT BUT BY PRAYER AND FASTING.

Matthew 17:19-21

It is of note that Jesus Christ did not embark on a new fasting and prayer season in order to drive out the devil. He had a lifestyle of fasting and prayer and was endued with power from on high. Without having even one extra day of fasting, Jesus Christ set the young man free from the power of darkness. Fasting and prayer is an important lifestyle for a spiritual person. A spiritual person cannot eat as much as everyone else and cannot engage in as much useless socializing as everyone else. Prayer releases the power of God because prayer invites God into your life and into your situation. Without inviting God into your life, you will never have God's power and involvement in your situation.

# CHAPTER 13

# Demonic Possession

And when he was come to the other side into the country of the Gergesenes, there met him two POSSESSED WITH DEVILS, coming out of the tombs, exceeding fierce, so that no man might pass by that way.

Matthew 8:28

**D**emonic possession occurs when the devil is in charge of a human being. You cannot be in charge of a human being until you control his mind. When the devil controls a human being, it causes demon possession.

Demonic possession comes along with many specific symptoms that are all indications of the presence of a devil. Here is a list of many of the symptoms and signs of demonic possession. These features show that demons actively assault the mind of a person with the hope of taking it over completely. It is when a person is taken over completely that he is possessed (owned).

Basically, it is safe to say that demonic possession causes madness. When the mind of an individual is owned by the devil, he is possessed. Let us now note some of the common characteristics of demonic possession. All the characteristics of demonic possession are seen in the mad man of Gadara whose condition was described in detail in the book of Mark. The Bible calls this condition "demon possession", whereas the medical profession calls this same mix of symptoms "schizophrenia".

1. **Demon possession is characterized by lots of fear.**

**Who had his DWELLING AMONG THE TOMBS; and no man could bind him, no, not with chains:**

**Mark 5:3**

A demon-possessed person lives a life of fear. He is frightened by the devil and lives in a state of fear and paranoia. Demon activity causes fear. God has not given us a spirit of fear. Fear is a spirit. Demon attacks on your mind lead to fear. The mad man of Gadara lived in a cemetery, which is the most frightening and solitary place a person could ever live in.

2.   **Demonic possession is characterized by stubbornness and delusions.**

**Because that he had been often bound with fetters and chains, and the chains had been plucked asunder by him, and the fetters broken in pieces: NEITHER COULD ANY MAN TAME HIM.**

**Mark 5:4**

A demon-possessed man is stubborn.  A demon-possessed person cannot be tamed.  Delusions make a person untameable.  Delusions are stubborn wrong beliefs.  Demon activity leads to strong stubborn beliefs in the wrong things.  Even when there is contrary evidence, people possessed with devils do not change their minds.  Failure to change the mind, in spite of contrary evidence is one of the major symptoms of mental illness.

3.   **Demonic possession is characterized by hallucinations.**

**And always, night and day, he was in the mountains, and in the tombs, crying, and cutting himself with stones.**

**Mark 5:5**

A demon-possessed man hears voices and sees things that other people do not.  The mad man of Gadara was hearing voices that were instructing him to cut himself with stones.  Demon-possessed people may hear voices accusing them, talking to them, advising them or insulting them.  They may see people and notice things that are not real and that do not exist at all.

Having hallucinations is experiencing something that does not exist.  A person may see things that are not real and hear things that are not real.  People experiencing a strong assault of demons on their mind start to hear and to see things that are not found in the physical realm.

**4.    Demonic possession is characterized by depression.**

**And always, night and day, he was in the mountains, and in the tombs, crying, and cutting himself with stones.**

**Mark 5:5**

A demon-possessed person is depressed.  The mad man of Gadara was constantly crying, weeping and wailing alone in the cemetery.  The person whose mind is under attack can experience very low seasons of sadness, a loss of hope, a loss of appetite, a lack of interest in life and a change in sleep patterns.

**5.    Demonic possession is characterized by much abnormal behaviour.**

**And when he was come to the other side into the country of the Gergesenes, there met him two POSSESSED WITH DEVILS, coming out of the tombs, exceeding fierce, so that no man might pass by that way.**

**Matthew 8:28**

A demon-possessed person exhibits a lot of abnormal behaviour.  The mad men of Gergesenes were violent.  They would not allow anyone to pass by their territory.  A person under attack from devils may experience negative symptoms where he shows little or no emotion (affective flattening), little or no speech (alogia) and little or no initiative, motivation or interest (avolition).  When a person has little or no emotion, he can easily become a murderer because he has little or no emotions for the people he kills or harms.

**6.    Demonic possession is characterized by social deterioration.**

**And they come to Jesus, and see him that was possessed with the devil, and had the legion, sitting, and CLOTHED, and in his right mind: and they were afraid.**

**Mark 5:15**

A demon-possessed person undergoes severe social deterioration. The mad man of Gadara deteriorated socially. He removed all his clothes and lived in a cemetery, away from society. A person under attack from devils may lose interest in self-care, his dressing and appearance, his work, his school and his very own life.

# CHAPTER 14

# Demonic Buffeting

And lest I should be exalted above measure through the abundance of the revelations, there was given to me a thorn in the flesh, THE MESSENGER OF SATAN TO BUFFET ME, lest I should be exalted above measure.

2 Corinthians 12:7

**D**emons are sometimes divinely allowed to have access to a saint of God for a specific purpose. There are a few examples of God allowing His people to be tempted, harassed and buffeted by evil spirits.

The devil is ready to steal, kill and destroy. Stealing, killing and destroying is a mindless reflex of a very wicked devil. Any access that satan has to God's people will result in senseless stealing, killing and destroying.

Satan could not help himself but to kill Jesus Christ on the cross, even though it led to satan's own defeat and destruction. All the devils in the mad man of Gadara could not restrain themselves from killing the very pigs they had entered. They destroyed their new accommodation of pigs as a reflex action. There are three well-known cases of satanic buffeting:

- Demonic buffeting in the life of the apostle Paul,

- Demonic buffeting in the life of Job and

- Demonic buffeting in the lives of the Corinthian fornicators.

### 1. Demonic Buffeting of Apostle Paul

Apostle Paul experienced buffeting in a terrible way. He prayed three times to the Lord for it to be taken away. Unfortunately, God did not choose to remove the messenger of satan on Paul's life. This messenger of satan was allowed to give Paul great difficulty, infirmity and weakness. This buffeting was manifested as a never-ending problem in the life of Paul. This was a problem that had the power to weaken and distress the apostle, but not enough to hinder his real ministry. There are many ministers who experience demonic buffeting on a regular basis. They have a problem that serves to keep them humble, yet they carry on effectively in the ministry. A personal talk with people like Apostle Paul will reveal how they are beset with serious weaknesses and problems. The most amazing thing is how they are able to carry on their God-given ministries with such problems in the background.

**And lest I should be exalted above measure through the abundance of the revelations, there was given to me a thorn in the flesh, THE MESSENGER OF SATAN TO BUFFET ME, lest I should be exalted above measure. For this thing I besought the Lord thrice, that it might depart from me. And he said unto me, My grace is sufficient for thee: for my strength is made perfect in weakness. Most gladly therefore will I rather glory in my infirmities, that the power of Christ may rest upon me.**

**2 Corinthians 12:7-9**

### 2. Demonic Buffeting of Job

Job is famous for his ability to survive demonic buffeting. He experienced buffeting in a terrible way. Such divinely allowed buffeting can and does produce sickness, death, robbery and tragedy. Satan was given limited access to Job in order to test him. The tests, however, were really severe and involved the death of his family and the destruction of his property and business. Job is famous for having survived this demonic buffeting that was permitted into his life.

**And the Lord said unto Satan, Hast thou considered my servant Job, that there is none like him in the earth, a perfect and an upright man, one that feareth God, and escheweth evil? And still he holdeth fast his integrity, although thou movedst me against him, to destroy him without cause. And Satan answered the Lord, and said, Skin for skin, yea, all that a man hath will he give for his life. But put forth thine hand now, and touch his bone and his flesh, and he will curse thee to thy face. And the Lord said unto Satan, BEHOLD, HE IS IN THINE HAND; BUT SAVE HIS LIFE. So went Satan**

forth from the presence of the Lord, and smote Job
with sore boils from the sole of his foot unto his crown.

**Job 2:3-7**

### 3.  Demonic Buffeting of the Corinthian Church

The Corinthian members who were engaged in fornication
with their relatives were also handed over to satan for buffeting.
In other words, satan was given special access to these Corinthians
who were having sex with their parents.  Of course, if satan is
given access to you, he will steal, kill and destroy.  Stealing,
killing and destroying is a reflex activity of satan.  Apostle Paul
spiritually removed the hedge from these individuals, knowing
very well that their flesh would be destroyed and they would die
prematurely.  Sometimes premature death is God's way of saving
you from total destruction.

In the name of our Lord Jesus Christ, when ye are
gathered together, and my spirit, with the power of our
Lord Jesus Christ, To deliver such an one unto Satan
for the DESTRUCTION OF THE FLESH, THAT
THE SPIRIT MAY BE SAVED in the day of the Lord
Jesus.

**1 Corinthians 5:4-5**

# CHAPTER 15

# Demonic Mixture

That THE SONS OF GOD saw the daughters of
men that they were fair; and they TOOK THEM
WIVES of all which they chose.

**Genesis 6:2**

**D**emonic mixture is when demon spirits blend with human flesh and produce parahumans and demonic hybrids that walk upon the earth, amongst human beings. This book is written to help you to understand your enemy in every form that he takes - whether it is devils, foul spirits or unclean hateful birds and creatures. This book is written to help you overcome the devil in any form that he takes. This book is written to help you fight evil spirits in every form or fashion.

In this chapter, you will understand how evil spirits have blended with human beings to form even more wicked parahumans and hybrids. A parahuman is a kind of human being who is not from the mainstream of human beings. A hybrid is simply a mixture of spirit and man or a mixture of spirit and animal. Let us go through the steps that describe this amazing phenomenon of demonic mixture.

1.    **DEMONIC MIXTURE: Fallen angels had sex with women creating half-angel, half-human creatures (PARAHUMANS).**

And it came to pass, when men began to multiply on the face of the ground, and daughters were born unto them, that the sons of God saw the daughters of men that they were fair; and they took them wives of all that they chose.

And Jehovah said, My spirit shall not strive with man for ever, for that he also is flesh: yet shall his days be a hundred and twenty years.

THE WERE GIANTS (NEPHILIM) IN THE EARTH IN THOSE DAYS, AND ALSO AFTER THAT, WHEN THE SONS OF GOD CAME UNTO THE DAUGHTERS OF MEN, AND THEY BARE CHILDREN TO THEM: THE SAME WERE THE MIGHTY MEN  (GIBBOR) THAT WERE OF OLD, THE MEN OF RENOWN (SEM).

And Jehovah saw that the wickedness of man was great in the earth, and that every imagination of the thoughts of his heart was only evil continually.  And it repented Jehovah that he had made man on the earth, and it grieved him at his heart. And Jehovah said, I will destroy man whom I have created from the face of the ground; both man, and beast, and creeping things, and birds of the heavens; for it repenteth me that I have made them.

But Noah found favor in the eyes of Jehovah.

Genesis 6:1-8 (ASV)

In the days of Noah, the sons of God (fallen angels, spiritual beings) invaded human beings through sex. This union of evil spirits and human beings brought forth three types of creatures: the Nephilim (giants), the Gibbor (tyrants) and the Sem (famous men).

**And it came to pass, when men began to multiply on the face of the earth, and daughters were born unto them, that the sons of God saw the daughters of men that they were fair; and they took them wives of all which they chose.**

**Genesis 6:1-2**

The concept of angels having sex with women is a biblical one. It is not an idea that is foreign to the Holy Bible. Some people feel that angels could not have had sexual intercourse.

As men have sought after God, satan has been provoked to jealousy. Satan is surprised that men everywhere are turning towards God. Satan is surprised that men desire to find their creator. Satan is filled with jealousy, hatred and madness because we love God. Satan desires to kill and destroy all creatures who love and serve God.

This combination of human beings and fallen angels produced a race of evil creatures who corrupted the earth. In the days leading up to the coming of Jesus, we can expect even more of exactly what happened in the days of Noah to happen again.

Human beings became evil because many of them were actually a combination of devil and man. There are many human beings who behave like devils. They steal, they kill and they destroy effortlessly and without feeling any pity.

The offspring of the angels and men were abnormal beings who became giants, bullies and unusual men of renown. Indeed, the products of the angels and the men were so unusual that they became famous. Today, the stories of these famous men of renown are still told all over the world. Their presence on earth and their deeds are unforgettable.

It is believed that some famous people with super human abilities in sports, athletics, politics and war are actually part angel and part human.

When evil enemies enter a city, they often burn down and destroy everything they can. Because satan cannot rule the creation, he seeks to destroy it.

There are several human beings who are actually half-devil and half-human. Satan is well known to be a murderer, a liar and a corrupter. The fallen angels have introduced corruption into the world. The half-devil half-human condition is even more deadly than a human being possessed with devils because in this case, a human being actually operates like the devil on earth. The devil has taken the infiltration of human beings one step further.

## The Book of Enoch

The Book of Enoch gives more detail than the Bible about the activities of fallen angels. The book of Genesis actually summarizes and quotes from the Book of Enoch. Fallen angels apparently did much more than have sex with women.

Indeed, you will discover that the first eight verses of the book of Genesis Chapter 6 are a summary of sixth, seventh and eighth chapters of what is known as the Book of Enoch. To get a more complete picture of the creation of demons, you will have to refer to the Book of Enoch which is another Christian book purported to be written by Enoch. I quote from this book just as I would quote from any other Christian author. You will notice that in many of my other books, I have quoted from other Christian authors. I know that many people consider the Book of Enoch as superior to ordinary Christian literature and even consider it as scripture. Indeed, the Book of Enoch is a full part of what is known as the Ethiopian Bible.

But to avoid controversy or even discussion, do not receive the Book of Enoch as scripture but as the writing of any other Christian scholar or believing author. The glimpses we have from the Bible are more than enough to paint the full picture for you. The notes from the Book of Enoch will only fill in the gaps to give you a better picture of what the Bible teaches. You will realise that eight verses of the Bible are actually a summary of twenty verses of the Book of Enoch and you will learn several important facts that are left out in the summarised version in the book of Genesis.

Read for yourself what the leader of the fallen angels, Semjaza, and his associates did to mankind.

**And the angels taught them charms and spells, and the cutting of roots, and made them acquainted with plants. ...And there was great impiety, they turned away from God, and committed fornication, and they were led astray, and became corrupt in all their ways.**

**Enoch 7:2, 8:2**

**Semjaza taught the casting of spells, and root-cuttings, Armaros taught counter-spells (release from spells), Baraqijal taught astrology, Kokabel taught the constellations (portents), Ezeqeel the knowledge of the clouds, Araqiel the signs of the earth, Shamsiel the signs of the sun, and Sariel the course of the moon. And as men perished, they cried, and their cry went up to heaven.**

**Enoch 8:3**

The corruption and destruction of human society is caused by the presence of dark angels who have fallen from glory and are bent on destroying all that God has made.

Through the blood of Jesus, God has redeemed us and saved us from being corrupted and owned by satan. It is our duty to preach the gospel and help people to be saved from the wicked influence of satan. It is our duty to minister the Word of God until we deliver mankind from these evil beings whose main goal is to destroy mankind.

2. **DEMONIC MIXTURE: Fallen angels had sex with animals creating half-angel, half-animal creatures (ANGEL-ANIMAL HYBRIDS).**

**And all of them together went and took wives for themselves, each choosing one for himself, and they began to go in to them and to defile themselves with sex with them...**

**And they began to sin against birds, and beasts, and reptiles, and fish, and to devour one another's flesh, and drank the blood.**

**Enoch 7:1, 5**

Angel-animal hybrids are a combination of angels and animals and will therefore produce some kind of supernatural and spiritual animal.

The angels sinned against the animals by having sex with them, which led to the formation of half-angel, half-animal hybrids. The Bible makes mention of a man-lion creature. The lion-like man who fought with one of the mighty men of David is a good example of this. The same passage mentions a lion, which is obviously different from the lion-like man (2 Samuel 23:20). This shows you that the lion-like men were different from actual lions. When a lion-like man dies, what do you think will happen to the spiritual part of that creature?

Daniel spake and said, I saw in my vision by night, and, behold, the four winds of the heaven strove upon the great sea. And four great beasts came up from the sea, diverse one from another.

The first was like A LION, AND HAD EAGLE'S WINGS: I beheld till the wings thereof were plucked, and it was lifted up from the earth, and made stand upon the feet as a man, and a man's heart was given to it.

And behold another beast, a second, like to A BEAR, AND IT RAISED UP ITSELF ON ONE SIDE, and it had three ribs in the mouth of it between the teeth of it: and they said thus unto it, Arise, devour much flesh.

After this I beheld, and lo another, like A LEOPARD, WHICH HAD UPON THE BACK OF IT FOUR WINGS OF A FOWL; THE BEAST HAD ALSO FOUR HEADS; and dominion was given to it.

After this I saw in the night visions, and behold A FOURTH BEAST, DREADFUL AND TERRIBLE, AND STRONG EXCEEDINGLY; AND IT HAD GREAT IRON TEETH: it devoured and brake in pieces, and stamped the residue with the feet of it: and it was diverse from all the beasts that were before it; and it had ten horns.

Daniel 7:2-7

"And Benaiah the son of Jehoiada, the son of a valiant man, of Kabzeel, who had done many acts, he slew TWO LIONLIKE MEN of Moab: he went down also and slew A LION in the midst of a pit in time of snow:" (2 Samuel 23:20)

The destruction and corruption of God's creation is one of satan's crimes. He will be punished for this. Watch out for people who destroy nature and creation. It is a sin to destroy what God has created.

In 1 Corinthians we learn that when you commit fornication, you sin against your body. "Flee fornication. Every sin that a man doeth is without the body; but he that committeth fornication sinneth against his own body" (1 Corinthians 6:18). Therefore, when the angels sinned against birds, beasts, reptiles and fish, they were committing fornication with them.

Also, the angels are believed to have made different species of animals have sex with each other, thereby creating unusual breeds. All these sins corrupted the animals and created unusual animal species. Satan organised the mixing up and the corrupting of different species of animals. The Book of Enoch teaches us that the fallen angels sinned against animals, birds, reptiles and fish.

The creatures that were created by the union of the fallen angels and animals were malevolent and full of evil. They introduced a high level of wickedness and corruption of flesh into the world. The "corruption of all flesh" is the contamination and the mixing up and the spoiling of the creation. Dinosaurs were a product of these unlawful mixtures of angel and animals and a mixture of other supernatural animals. Did you know that dinosaurs are actually a combination of reptiles and birds? Dinosaurs have hollow bones like birds and a pelvic structure. Dinosaurs look and act like giant lizards and crocodiles. The large size of these dinosaurs is a symptom of angelic involvement with the animals! Films like *Jurassic Park* reveal the nature of these mixed and corrupted creatures that once lived on the earth. If you watch the film, *Jurassic Park* you will see how the dinosaurs were a mixture of flying birds and reptiles.

Remember that when angels had sex with men, large sized men (giants) were created. It is probably the angelic involvement with the animals that led to the huge sizes of these animals. These super animals are both spiritual and physical creatures. This must not sound so strange to you as many people do have sex with animals today.

*The corruption of the creation was produced by the union between angels and men, angels and animals, men and animals, and unions of different species of animals.*

3. **DEMONIC MIXTURE: Unclean Spirits (spirits which resemble unclean animals) were formed by the combination of angels with animals and further combinations of animal hybrids with other animals.**

And saw heaven opened, and a certain vessel descending unto him, as it had been a great sheet knit at the four corners, and let down to the earth: Wherein were ALL MANNER OF FOURFOOTED BEASTS OF THE EARTH, AND WILD BEASTS, AND CREEPING THINGS, AND FOWLS OF THE AIR.

And there came a voice to him, Rise, Peter; kill, and eat. But Peter said, Not so, Lord; for I have never eaten any thing that is common or UNCLEAN. And the voice spake unto him again the second time, what God hath cleansed, that call not thou common.

**Acts 10:11-15**

And I saw three unclean spirits like frogs come out of the mouth of the dragon, and out of the mouth of the beast, and out of the mouth of the false prophet.

**Revelation 16:13**

In the scripture above, Peter describes a host of different unclean animals. Unclean animals are a group of animals Moses said were not to be eaten. All through the Bible, you hear about "unclean" spirits. These must be spirits that resemble the list of unclean animals. This is why they are called "unclean" spirits.

Unclean spirits are just like the group of animals such as reptiles, amphibians, birds and horses, which Jews could not eat. There is only one scripture that describes an unclean spirit and it describes it as a frog.

All through the Bible, you will read about unclean spirits in the dark world that resemble animals. There is enough evidence in the Scripture to make us know that there are evil spirits that have animal features. Where do these animal spirits come from? Did God create them? How were they created? That is what this chapter seeks to explain. Did God intentionally create these evil creatures? There are spiritually evil animals out there and they are mentioned time and time again throughout the Bible.

Unclean spirits, which are animal spirits were created by fallen angels having intercourse with animals and the products of this union continuing to have intercourse with one another. The fallen angels sinned against birds and animals, fish and reptiles. By having sex with these animals, they produced offspring, which continue to have intercourse with each other. This kind of intercourse produced strange wicked spirit-animal creatures which we know as "unclean (animal) spirits".

(The fallen angels also taught men magic, witchcraft and how to cast spells. You will notice that places in which there is a lot of idol worship and demon activity there is usually incest, witchcraft, magic and the casting of spells. The idols they worship are usually exact images of the demons. This is why the word "demon" is also translated "deity" or "god".) Notice this passage from the Book of Enoch:

**AND ALL OF THEM TOGETHER WENT AND TOOK WIVES FOR THEMSELVES, EACH CHOOSING ONE FOR HIMSELF, AND THEY BEGAN TO GO IN TO THEM AND TO DEFILE THEMSELVES WITH SEX WITH THEM,**

**AND THE ANGELS TAUGHT THEM CHARMS AND SPELLS, and the cutting of roots, and made them acquainted with plants.**

**And the women became pregnant, and they bare large giants, whose height was three thousand cubits (ells).**

**The giants consumed all the work and toil of men. And when men could no longer sustain them, the giants turned against them and devoured mankind.**

**And THEY BEGAN TO SIN AGAINST BIRDS, AND BEASTS, AND REPTILES, AND FISH, AND TO DEVOUR ONE ANOTHER'S FLESH, AND DRANK THE BLOOD.**

**Then the earth laid accusation against the lawless ones.**

**Enoch 7: 1-6**

What happens when half-animal half-angel creatures die? Obviously, these half-angel / half animal creatures would have to continue existing because angels are spirits.

When these grotesque half-angel / half-animal creatures died, their spirits, which were a bizarre merger of angels and animals, lived on in the realm of darkness. If they had been just animals, they would have died like ordinary animals and disappeared into the earth's lifecycle. But because they were a combination of animals and angels, they continued to live on in the spirit realm of darkness. ("Darkness" is a term for a realm that cannot be seen).

There are many of such creatures in the "dark world" around your house and around where you live. They were there before you were born and they have no intention of going anywhere. If you picture these creatures living in and around your house, it will spur you on to rise up and pray to bind their activities and prevent them from their operations and manoeuvres in your life.

The demons I am talking about are a completely different kind of spiritual being. They are hybrids of fallen wicked angels and animals. They are hybrid spirits. This is why they have a completely different name in the Greek language. In the Greek language, they are called *diamonions*. *Diamonion* means a deity and an evil spirit.

Mermaids, for instance, are human-fish combinations. I know of people who have encountered half-woman / half-fish creatures.

Moloch was the name of the idol god of the Ammonites to which human victims, especially children, were offered in sacrifice. Its image was a brazen figure with the head of a goat and outstretched human arms. All through the Old Testament you will find God admonishing His children not to follow the evil practices of the heathen that included worshipping the images of demons.

**Yea, ye took up the tabernacle of Moloch, and the star of your god Remphan, figures which ye made to worship them: and I will carry you away beyond Babylon.**

**Acts 7:43**

Have you noticed that famous idols and deities throughout history have grotesque shapes and features of human-animal combinations? Human beings are taught by demons to make these idols and worship them. *Idols are often images of creatures that exist in the spirit realm.* Satan longs for human beings to worship him. Satan wants to take attention away from God. These demonic creatures exist in the darkness and these are what we are actually fighting against when we engage in spiritual warfare.

These creatures, which are depicted in ancient art, actually look like evil creatures described in the Bible. An example of such a creature can be found in the book of Revelation - "And I stood upon the sand of the sea, and saw a beast rise up out of the sea, having seven heads and ten horns, and upon his horns ten crowns, and upon his heads the name of blasphemy. . . And I beheld another beast coming up out of the earth; and he had two horns like a lamb, and he spake as a dragon" (Revelation 13:1, 11). Any time you are dealing with evil entities and beings in prayer, you must picture these creatures as what you are actually fighting against.

**But I say, that the things which the Gentiles sacrifice, they sacrifice to devils, and not to God: and I would not that ye should have fellowship with devils.**

**1 Corinthians 10:20**

These creatures want to be worshipped and cause men to create images of themselves. This is why many of the idols of our world look like these half-human half-animal entities. Idol worshippers are forced to carve out these creatures and worship them. Indeed, the word "demon" in the Bible is the word "deity" which actually means a god. Often when you sacrifice to idols, you are sacrificing to demons.

# CHAPTER 16

# Examples of Demon-Animal Hybrids

These demon-animal hybrids are well known idols in history, art and culture. This is why you must be careful about bringing images and artefacts which you do not really understand into your home. Many of these myths are pictures of demon-animal hybrids that actually existed and were worshipped. Satan's aim is always to be worshipped instead of God. He wants to replace God and be worshipped. In creating these grotesque creatures and beings, he gives human beings something to look up to and something to worship.

## MOLOCH

Moloch was half-human, half-goat and one of the false gods that Israel would worship during its periods of apostasy. One of the practices of the worshippers of Moloch was to sacrifice their children.

## MINOTAUR

The Minotaur was half-man, half-bull and is often depicted with a man's body and bull's head. This was said to be the product of Queen Pasiphae's strange lust for a bull. The result of this union was the Minotaur.

## LEDA

This picture shows a swan seducing Queen Leda, ( Leda was the mother of Hellen of Troy) to produce an abomination.

## ACHILLES

This picture shows Achilles who was said to be a brave handsome warrior and was the product of Peleus and a sea nymph.

## ECHIDNA

This picture shows Echidna who was a half-woman, half-serpent monster. She ate men raw. Greek mythology has it that Echidna was the daughter of Phorcys and Ceto. She coupled with another half-snake, Typhon, and gave birth to Hydra, Cerberus, and Chimaera.

## MEDUSA

The picture shows Medusa, described as a woman with living venomous snakes in place of hair.

## SPHINX

Sphinx is the half-bird, half-woman creature.

It was known to have dwelt at a mountain entrance. It would ask travellers a riddle, and if they failed, she would eat them.

## CENTAUR

The Centaur was a race of creatures which are part human and part horse.

## AMUN

Amun is an Egyptian god portrayed as a man with a ram head.

## ANUBIS

Anubis is the Egyptian name for a jackal-headed god associated with mummification and the afterlife in Egyptian mythology.

## BASTET

The goddess Bastet was usually represented as a woman with the head of a domesticated cat.

## CHIMAERA

The Chimaera was a fire-breathing beast with a lion's head and body, a serpent for a tail, and a goat's head in the midsection. The chimaera ravaged Mount Chimaera and was eventually killed by the hero Bellerophon, who shot lead into its mouth. The lead melted in its fiery breath and burnt its insides.

## HORUS

Horus is a god with the head of a falcon and the body of a human. The kings of Egypt associated themselves with Horus. Horus was among the most important gods of Egypt, particularly because the Pharaoh was supposed to be his earthly embodiment.

**And as were the days of Noah, so shall be the coming of the Son of man.**

**Matthew 24:37 (NIV)**

We are in the last days! Perhaps we are in the last hours of the last days! As it was in the days of Noah, so shall the coming of the Son of man be. The conditions that were prevailing in the days of Noah will be the conditions we will experience when the Son of man returns. The world will have gone full cycle and returned to the state that Noah found it in.

What did Noah experience? What were the conditions prevailing at the time of Noah? Jesus told us that in Noah's time, men were eating and drinking, marrying and being given in marriage, completely oblivious to God's will.

**For as in those days which were before the flood they were eating and drinking, marrying and giving in marriage, until the day that Noah entered into the ark,**

**and they knew not until the flood came, and took them all away; so shall be the coming of the Son of man.**

**Matthew 24:38-39**

But there is much more to the days of Noah than what is mentioned in the twenty-fourth chapter of Matthew. The reason for the flood was the wickedness of human beings. There was great evil in the world. Great wickedness was established in the human race. In the days before Noah, men had abnormal sex and gave birth to human-animal hybrids. Today, people are seeking for licences to marry animals.

I recently asked my mother if the world was more evil today than when she was a young girl in the 1940s. She answered and said, "The world is far more evil today than when I was a young girl."

Actually, it is quite easy to see that the world is more evil today than it used to be. If you take a look at films that were made thirty years ago, you will see a clear difference in the level of wickedness in the films. Movies are always a reflection of real life and real things that happen in this world. The style, the frequency and the extent of killing that is depicted in movies today are on a completely different scale to movies that were made thirty years ago. Indeed, the movies of today reveal the huge advances that have been made in human wickedness. Higher dimensions of fornication, prostitution, adultery, homosexuality, murder, rape, robberies, betrayal, genocide, fighting, brutality, wickedness and all forms of war are portrayed clearly in our movies today. Sixty per cent of all internet traffic is pornography and about seventy per cent of all men watch pornography regularly.

**And Jehovah saw that THE WICKEDNESS OF MAN WAS GREAT IN THE EARTH, and that every imagination of the thoughts of his heart was only evil continually.**

**Genesis 6:5**

As it was in the days of Noah, we can expect the wickedness of men to increase greatly. We can expect murder, immorality and homosexuality to multiply a thousand-fold. The days of Noah are the days of the maturity of evil.

# CHAPTER 17

# How Super-Humans/ Para-Humans Were Created

IN THOSE DAYS, and even afterward, GIANTS LIVED ON THE EARTH, for whenever the sons of God had intercourse with human women, they gave birth to children who became the heroes mentioned in legends of old.

**Genesis 6:4 (NLT)**

**B**ut is there any biblical basis for the existence of people who seem to be para-normal or super-normal in any way? Does the Bible speak about super-normal, abnormal or parahuman beings? Is there any mention of half-human half-animal beings? Yes, there is! There is a lot in the scripture that teaches about the existence of such beings.

> **There were GIANTS (NEPHILIM) in the earth in those days; and also after that, when the sons of God came in unto the daughters of men, and they bare children to them, the same became mighty MEN (GIBBORIM) which were of old, MEN OF RENOWN (SEM).**
>
> **Genesis 6:4**

From the Bible, we learn that angels had sex with human beings and this introduced unusual creatures into the world. These unusual creatures are what we call *parahumans*. The Hebrew language gives three different names for these three different types of creatures. The *Nephilim*, the *Gibbor* and the *Sem*.

These three types of super para-humans introduced a lot of evil into the world.

The *Nephilims* were the giants. The giants were oversized men who were very tall and huge. In those days of hunting and fighting, the huge size was of a great advantage. However, with advancing technology, the great size was not very helpful.

The *Gibbor* were tyrants or mighty men who were not necessarily giants. They were men of normal size, but very wicked, powerful and with great influence. Some of the great wicked men of our time could easily have been *Gibbors*. Adolf Hitler, Genghis Khan and Joseph Stalin could easily have been *Gibbors*.

The *Sem* were famous people or men of renown. There were many people who did things that made them famous. Today, there are athletes, singers, boxers, who achieve things that are on the fringes of human capability.

These three groups of super humans introduced a lot of wickedness that became widespread throughout the world. Three different kinds of evil beings were now set loose on the earth.

Human history is full of stories of giants, tyrants, bullies and men of unimaginable wickedness who have lived on this earth. Our human history describes many people who once lived and never showed anyone the slightest bit of human kindness or compassion. Many of these wicked people were super para-humans. Even today, we can see the most brutal inhuman treatment of fellow human beings by other men. You wonder whether it is normal human beings who are inflicting such wickedness on their fellow humans. Do they not have any feelings? Do they not care at all?

All through history, people have asked the question, "Do these tyrants not have any feelings when they were torturing their fellow man?" The reason why many of these people do not have feelings is because they are half human and half fallen angel. Half spirit and half man!

Do not over react to the idea of someone being half spirit and half man. Jesus Christ Himself was born of the Virgin Mary. Jesus was half human and half non-human because He was born of a virgin and not from the seed of a man. He was a God-man. You can see that He had super-normal abilities. It is only natural to expect that someone who is not really a human being will be super-human.

The record of this world-changing event of angels having sex with human beings and creating super humans is only briefly mentioned in the book of Genesis. It is also referred to in the books of Jude and Peter. The record of this event originally came from the Book of Enoch, from where it seems to have been originally quoted.

Let us now go through the stages that led to the existence of super para-humans and the eventual creation of demons as we know them today.

## Steps to the Creation of Super Humans
## (*Sem, Gibbor, Nephilim*)

1. Angels fall from heaven by following Lucifer in rebellion against God.

   ... Satan, which deceiveth the whole world: he was cast out into the earth, *and HIS ANGELS* WERE CAST OUT WITH HIM.

   Revelation 12:9

2. Fallen angels take up positions on earth and become princes of this world.

   Which none of the PRINCES OF THIS WORLD knew: for had they known it, they would not have crucified the Lord of glory.

   1 Corinthians 2:8

3. Some of the fallen angels on earth spy beautiful women on earth and desire to have sex with them.

   And it came to pass, when men began to multiply on the face of the earth, and daughters were born unto them, that the sons of God saw the daughters of men that they were fair; and they took them wives of all which they chose.

   Genesis 6:1-2

Supernatural beings, called sons of God, had sex with beautiful women and gave birth to abnormal creatures who were called giants and *Nephilims*. We assume these "sons of God" to be fallen angels because satan is associated with them in the book of Job.

Even though the angels had fallen away from the glory of God, some of the fallen angels fell deeper into depravity. Among the fallen angels, there was a group that were really sinful and fell even further away from God. This is the group of angels that had sex with human beings. After seeing the beautiful women in the world, some of the fallen angels took a quality decision to go further and actually experience what human beings were experiencing in sexual intercourse. This decision was taken by a group of two hundred fallen angels. This event is recorded in the Book of Enoch.

This event of angels having sex should not strike you as strange because all through the Bible, angels take on the form of human beings and do things that human beings do such as eating, drinking and sleeping.

This event is also recorded in the book of Jude, which many believe is from the Book of Enoch. "And the angels which kept not their first estate, but left their own habitation, he hath reserved in everlasting chains under darkness unto the judgment of the great day" (Jude 1:6).

In the Book of Enoch we are even given the names of the angels that decided to go down and have sex with the human race. You can compare the account in the Book of Enoch to the account in the book of Genesis. We are given the name of the leader of these angels who decided to leave their estate in heaven and descend into further depravity.

**When the human population began to grow rapidly on the earth,**

**the sons of God saw the beautiful women of the human race and took any they wanted as their wives.**

**Then the LORD said, "My Spirit will not put up with humans for such a long time, for they are only mortal flesh. In the future, they will live no more than 120 years."**

**In those days, and even afterward, giants lived on the earth, for whenever the sons of God had intercourse with human women, they gave birth to children who became the heroes mentioned in legends of old.**

Now the LORD observed the extent of the people's wickedness, and he saw that all their thoughts were consistently and totally evil.

So the LORD was sorry he had ever made them. It broke his heart.

And the LORD said, "I will completely wipe out this human race that I have created. Yes, and I will destroy all the animals and birds, too. I am sorry I ever made them."

But Noah found favor with the LORD.

**Genesis 6:1-8 (NLT)**

And it came to pass when the children of men had multiplied that in those days were born to them beautiful and fair daughters.

And the angels, the sons of heaven, saw and lusted after them, and said to one another: 'Come, let us choose us wives from among the children of men

And have children with them.' And SEMJAZA, WHO WAS THEIR LEADER, said to them: 'I fear you will not agree to do this deed,

And I alone shall have to pay the penalty of this great sin.'

And they all answered him and said: 'Let us all swear an oath, and all bind ourselves by mutual curses so we will not abandon this plan but to do this thing.' Then they all swore together and bound themselves by mutual curses.

And THEY WERE IN ALL TWO HUNDRED who descended in the days of Jared in the summit of Mount Hermon, and they called it Mount Hermon, because they had sworn and bound themselves by mutual curses on the act.

And THESE ARE THE NAMES OF THEIR LEADERS: Samlazaz, their leader, Araklba, Rameel, Kokablel, Tamlel, Ramlel, Danel, Ezeqeel, Baraqijal,

*[Author's note: Samlazaz could be another spelling of Semjaza, and possibly be the same entity]*

**Asael, Armaros, Batarel, Ananel, Zaqiel, Samsapeel, Satarel, Turel, Jomjael, Sariel. These are their chiefs of tens.**

**Enoch 6:1-8**

## 4. Fallen angels teach human beings many evil things and introduce bloodshed, casting of spells and other forms of wickedness into the human race.

In the Book of Enoch the specific angels which taught particular evil things were mentioned. It is important to realise that great evil has been introduced into our world by the presence of fallen angels. The complex array of sins and the complicated mystery of iniquity can only be explained by the presence of these gruesome wicked creatures in our midst. Iniquity is a mystery because it can hardly be explained by any straight-thinking person.

Many of the things that men practice today were actually introduced by fallen angels. These things have served to multiply wickedness among mankind. Men were taught to make weapons that would be used to kill each other. Men were taught to adorn and beautify themselves in order to lead men into more fornication and immorality. Men were taught about witchcraft, astrology, casting of spells and the use of herbs and drugs. Indeed, many of the things we take for granted today are actually evils that were introduced into our world by fallen angels.

**And Azazel taught men to make swords, and knives, and shields, and breastplates, and taught them about metals of the earth and the art of working them, and bracelets, and ornaments, and the use of antimony, and the beautifying of the eyelids, and all kinds of precious stones, and all coloring and dyes.**

**And there was great impiety, they turned away from God, and committed fornication, and they were led astray, and became corrupt in all their ways.**

Semjaza taught the casting of spells, and root-cuttings, Armaros taught counter-spells (release from spells), Baraqijal taught astrology, Kokabel taught the constellations (portents), Ezeqeel the knowledge of the clouds, Araqiel the signs of the earth, Shamsiel the signs of the sun, and Sariel the course of the moon. And as men perished, they cried, and their cry went up to heaven.

And the women have borne giants, and the whole earth has thereby been filled with blood and unrighteousness.

**Enoch 8:1-3, 9:9**

5.    Fallen angels have sex with beautiful women and give birth to half angel-half humans called "*NEPHILIMS*" (GIANTS).

There were GIANTS (*NEPHILIM*) in the earth in those days; and also after that, when the sons of God came in unto the daughters of men, and they bare children to them, the same became mighty MEN (*GIBBOR*) which were of old, MEN OF RENOWN (*SEM*).

**Genesis 6:4**

Three types of para-humans were created by the union of fallen angel and human being. The first type of para-human was the *NEPHILIM*. These nephilims were giants or oversized men. When the angels had sex with the beautiful ladies, they became pregnant and gave birth to half-angel half-human babies.

Perhaps, your immediate response to the idea of angels having sex would be to laugh. But you must remember that even though Jesus said that angels do not marry, He did not say they could not have sex. Many people have sex even though they are not married. Obviously, these angels had sex organs and were able to copulate with human women.

The giants created by the combination of angels and men were large sized men who, by their virtual size, dominated the world.

In the primitive world, to be a large size was to be superior. Your size alone would give you the upper hand in any fight. This is why Goliath was such a great threat to the Israelites. These giants became brutally wicked and were well-known for their bullying and brutish behaviour. Remember that these giants were half-fallen angel and half-human.

These products of a super-human race combining with a human race produced unusual creatures. These unusual creatures had the form of super-human/super-normal men, having six rows of fingers, six rows of toes and two rows of teeth. They were fearful, grotesque, terrifying creatures to encounter.

It is no wonder that the Israelites were afraid to enter the Promised Land because of the giants. When Moses led the Israelites into the Promised Land, the ten spies saw these giants and were terrified. The spies were not making up a story when they said that there were giants in the land. There were real literal giants that they had to deal with. David also had to fight with the giant called Goliath. Goliath had brothers who were also giants. These are stories that sound fantastic today, but they happened.

Amazingly, a little research will reveal that every race on the earth has records in its history of the days when the giants lived on earth. Stories like *Jack and the Beanstalk*, *Gulliver's Travels* and *Hercules* come from the reality that giants once lived in the earth. Even in Ghana, there are stories of a famous giant called Asebu Amenfi who once lived amongst the people.

God's anger against the giants and the wickedness they brought to the earth is what led to Noah's flood. Amazingly, almost every group of people on earth has a story of a great flood in its history. The details of the story are slightly different but the basic line is that there was a massive flood that killed everybody and left a few people and some animals. Australia, Babylon, Burma; Guyana, Iceland, Canada, Greece, India, Italy, Mexico, Alaska, Russia and Hawaii have legends and stories about a great flood that came to the earth. Several of the stories indicate that God warned man.

6.    **Fallen angels have sex with beautiful women and give birth to half fallen angel-half humans called "***SEM***" (FAMOUS MEN).**

**There were GIANTS (*NEPHILIM*) in the earth in those days; and also after that, when the sons of God came in unto the daughters of men, and they bare children to them, the same became mighty MEN (*GIBBOR*) which were of old, MEN OF RENOWN (*SEM*).**

**Genesis 6:4**

The second type of parahumans created by the combination of fallen angels and human beings were called the "*SEM*". The "*SEM*" were simply famous people. Their fame was created by their special abilities. Such people would have super-human abilities. What did they do and what did they achieve that gave them notoriety and made them famous? To answer that, just ask yourself - what makes people famous today?

Some people are famous because of their inventions. Others are famous because of what they build. Some are famous because of the wars they win. Others are famous musicians, famous actors, famous athletes, famous singers, famous sportsmen, famous fighters, famous murderers, famous serial killers, famous men without feeling. Some are even famous because of their pornographic and sexual exploits and capabilities.

Indeed, some famous people you hear about may not be normal human beings but actually the *SEM*. Some women you may meet are actually super-human in their sexual exploits and behaviour.

## The Disappearing Super-humans

Are there people who are not really "people"? One Thursday evening, after church, the crowds were milling around in the car park as usual. One of my church members, a lawyer, sat in her car, turned the engine on and began to drive out of the car park.

Just before she drove out of the gate, a young lady who appeared to have attended the service asked her for a lift.

"Are you going this way?" the lawyer asked. The young girl nodded and the lady lawyer asked her to jump into the back of the car and they drove away from the church. When they had gone about two kilometres, the lady lawyer felt that the young girl was unusually quiet. So she looked back to ask if the young girl was okay. She received the shock of her life when she found that the young girl was not in the car. She had vanished into thin air! The lady lawyer was terrified because an apparently real human being who had entered her car a few minutes before had simply disappeared into nothingness. Indeed, it was a terrible experience for her and I had to go to her house to calm her down and pray for protection against every strange entity that wanted to attack her. It was a night I will never forget. I realised that there are people who are not "people"!

## The "Fish Woman"

One day, a church member told me about how an experience he had when he was not yet saved. He had met a beautiful girl who was happy to come and stay with him for a weekend. He said that from the word go, he noticed something unusual about the girl. Every time he offered her some food, she said that she was fasting. He found this unusual but she was willing to have sex with him like a normal girlfriend would.

On the second night with this young girl, he woke up and reached out to begin fondling his new lover who was fasting all the time. He began fondling her from her chest downwards and under the sheets. When his hand got towards her thighs he felt something wet and cold. He was startled and decided to look under the sheets. There, he received the most terrifying shock of his life. From the lady's waist downwards, she was a fish, sort of like a large tuna! He stared in disbelief and realised he was in bed with a "fish woman". Wouldn't you be scared if you realised that the lady you were in bed with was not a real human being?

Later that day, the lady who seemed to have turned back into a normal human being, gave him a warning. "You must never mention what you saw last night." She walked out of his house and he never saw her again. This testimony is another example of human beings who are not real human beings. They are what I call "para-humans"!

The big difference between the *SEM* and the *NEPHILIM* is that *NEPHILIMS* were giant sized men whereas *SEM* were normal sized but famous men. It is obvious that the *NEPHILIM* would become extinct because of its large size. The *SEM*, however, would be able to live on and persist unnoticed.

Today, we do not have giants but we do have many famous people with super-normal and para-human abilities. We have runners, boxes, singers, actors and murderers with unusual abilities. Dinosaurs are also extinct because of their large size but we do have a persistence of snakes, ants, antelopes, cats, dogs and lions which are of a more manageable size. Anything that is extremely large, becomes an easy target for extinction.

7. **Fallen angels have sex with beautiful women and give birth to half angel-half humans called "*GIBBOR*" (TYRANTS AND BULLIES).**

**There were GIANTS (*NEPHILIM*) in the earth in those days; and also after that, when the sons of God came in unto the daughters of men, and they bare children to them, the same became MIGHTY MEN (*GIBBOR*) which were of old, MEN OF RENOWN (*SEM*).**

**Genesis 6:4**

The third type of para-human that was created were the *GIBBOR*. Remember that these are different Hebrew words that mean different things. The word *Gibbor* means "tyrant". A "tyrant" is a ruler who uses power oppressively, unjustly or despotically. We have had several examples of this kind of person on earth. When these tyrants died, the fallen angels and their offspring became the demons in the world.

In modern times, men like Hannibal, Adolf Hitler, Stalin, Julius Caesar, Caligula were tyrants and bullies who were well-known for their merciless lives of wickedness. It is most likely that these people are remnants of the *Gibbor* that are continuing to exist on earth.

## Bullies and Tyrants

Many men without feelings and human compassion have lived amongst us. Lenin, the founder of communism, made an announcement, "It is necessary - urgently and secretly, to prepare the terror." He sent telegrams to introduce mass terror. This is one of his telegrams:

*"Comrades! The kulak uprising in your five districts must be crushed without pity ... You must make example of these people. (1) Hang (I mean hang publicly, so that people see it) at least 100 kulaks, rich bastards, and known bloodsuckers. (2) Publish their names. (3) Seize all their grain. (4) Single out the hostages per my instructions in yesterday's telegram. Do all this so that for miles around people see it all, understand it, tremble, and tell themselves that we are killing the bloodthirsty kulaks and that we will continue to do so ... Yours, Lenin. P.S. Find tougher people."*

There were numerous reports that the police and the interrogators utilized gruesome torture methods. You ask yourself if these people had any feelings of pity in them as they killed and tortured fellow human beings in the most inhumane way.

At Odessa, officers were slowly fed into furnaces or tanks of boiling water.

In Kharkiv, scalpings and hand-flayings were commonplace: the skin was peeled off victims' hands to produce "gloves". They would burn the victim's hands in boiling water until the blistered skin could be peeled off: this left the victims with raw and bleeding hands and their torturers with "human gloves".

Naked people were rolled around in barrels studded internally with nails; victims were crucified or stoned to death at Dnipropetrovsk.

At Kremenchuk members of the clergy were impaled and peasants were buried alive. In Orel, water was poured on naked prisoners bound in the winter streets until they became living ice statues. In Armavir they crushed their skulls by tightening a leather strap with an iron bolt around their head.

In Kiev, rats were placed in iron tubes sealed at one end with wire netting and the other placed against the body of a prisoner, with the tubes being heated until the rats gnawed through the victim's body in an effort to escape.

The Nazis, under Adolf Hitler, seemed to have no human feelings. When some people tried to overthrow Hitler, the conspirators were soon found out and punished. They were filmed whilst they were tortured to death. Some were strangled and others were hanged from meat hooks or by piano strings in front of a movie camera.

It was this kind of generalized evil that led to Noah's flood. God was forced to wipe out evil from the earth by drowning all the para-humans and the contaminated human race. All that I have said above is summarised in eight verses of the Bible. All that I have said above is also a summary of twenty verses of the Book of Enoch. The Book of Enoch and the book of Genesis are important to Christians because of these important revelations. These two books help to explain the presence of evil spirits as well as the presence of evil men. These texts give an explanation of what led to the creation of these evil beings.

8.   **God sends a flood to wipe out the *Nephilims* (giants), *Gibbors* (tyrants and bullies) and *Sems* (famous men).**

**And God looked upon the earth, and, behold, it was corrupt; for all flesh had corrupted his way upon the earth. And God said unto Noah, The end of all flesh is come before me; for the earth is filled with violence**

**through them; and, behold, I will destroy them with the earth.**

**Genesis 6:12-13**

As wickedness multiplied in the earth through the presence of para-humans, God decided to wipe out the entire creation and start all over again. When the flood came, all human beings, all giants, all famous men and all bullies were drowned. The world was left with Noah and his three sons. There were no more giants, tyrants and bullies because everything had been destroyed. All the *Gibbors*, *Sems* and *Nephilims* were completely wiped out.

**Then said the Most High, the Great and Holy One, Uriel go to the son of Lamech.**

**Say to him: 'Go to Noah and tell him in my name "Hide yourself!" and reveal to him the end that is approaching: that the whole earth will be destroyed, and a flood is about to come on the whole earth, and will destroy everything on it.'**

**Enoch 10:1-2**

9. **The *Nephilims* (giants), the *Gibbors* (tyrants and bullies) and the *Sems* (famous men) re-appear on the earth after the flood.**

However, many years after the great flood, which wiped out the *Gibbors*, the *Sems* and the *Nephilims*, we still read about giants being on earth. Below is a long list of giants that we read about in the Bible long after the flood. This is a worrying phenomenon because it appears that the *Gibbors*, *Sems*, and *Nephilims* found a way to survive during the flood. Let's have a look at the list of well-known giants that existed after Noah's flood.

*Ahiman:* "And Caleb drove thence the three SONS OF ANAK, Sheshai, and AHIMAN, and Talmai, the children of Anak" (Joshua 15:14).

*Anak:* "And they brought up an evil report of the land which they had searched unto the children of Israel, saying, The land, through which we have gone to search it, is a land that eateth up the inhabitants thereof; and all the people that we saw in it are men of a great stature.

And there we saw the giants, the sons of Anak, which come of the giants: and we were in our own sight as grasshoppers, and so we were in their sight" (Numbers 13:32-33)

*Arba:* "They gave these cities which are here mentioned by name from the tribe of the sons of Judah and from the tribe of the sons of Simeon; and they were for the sons of Aaron, one of the families of the Kohathites, of the sons of Levi, for the lot was theirs first.

Thus they gave them Kiriath- arba, ARBA BEING THE FATHER OF ANAK (that is, Hebron), in the hill country of Judah, with its surrounding pasture lands" (Joshua 21:9-11 NASB).

*Goliath:* "And there went out a champion out of the camp of the Philistines, named Goliath, of Gath, whose height was six cubits and a span.

And he had an helmet of brass upon his head, and he was armed with a coat of mail; and the weight of the coat was five thousand shekels of brass" (1 Samuel 17:4-5).

*Ishbibenob:* "And Ishbibenob, which was of the sons of the giant, the weight of whose spear weighed three hundred shekels of brass in weight, he being girded with a new sword, thought to have slain David" (2 Samuel 21:16).

*Lahmi:* "And there was war again with the Philistines; and Elhanan the son of Jair slew Lahmi the brother of Goliath the Gittite, whose spear staff was like a weaver's beam" (1 Chronicles 20:5).

*Saph:* "And it came to pass after this, that there was again a battle with the Philistines at Gob: then Sibbechai the Hushathite slew Saph, which was of the sons of the giant" (2 Samuel 21:18).

*Sheshai:* "And Caleb drove thence the three sons of Anak, SHESHAI, and Ahiman, and Talmai, THE CHILDREN OF ANAK" (Joshua 15:14).

*Talmai:* "And Caleb drove thence the three sons of Anak, Sheshai, and Ahiman, and TALMAI, the children of Anak" (Joshua 15:14).

*Og:* "For only Og king of Bashan remained of the remnant of giants; behold, his bedstead was a bedstead of iron; is it not in Rabbath of the children of Ammon? Nine cubits was the length thereof, and four cubits the breadth of it, after the cubit of a man" (Deuteronomy 3:11).

*A giant from Gath:* "Again there was war at Gath, where there was a man of great stature who had twenty- four fingers and toes, six fingers on each hand and six toes on each foot; and he also was descended from the giants" (1 Chronicles 20:6 NASB).

So why and how did giants re-surface after the flood? How did these giants reappear after the flood had apparently killed all of them? There is an answer to this mystery! *Apparently, when the flood came, the evil spirits of these combined fallen angels/human beings came out of the giants and creatures and waited for the waters to subside.* When men began to multiply on the earth again, the evil spirits invaded them producing giants and abnormal people. There is another book I want us to refer to that gives an even more detailed account of what happened. Let us now turn to an extract from *"Angels and Demons: From Creation to Armageddon"* by Joseph Lumpkin to read an even more detailed account of Noah's flood and how the demons came back into our world.

**"And the Lord opened seven floodgates of heaven, and He opened the mouths of the fountains of the great deep, seven mouths in number. And the floodgates began to pour down water from the heaven forty days and forty closets (nights). And the fountains of the deep**

also sent up waters, until the whole world was full of water.

The waters increased on the earth, by fifteen cubits (a cubit is about 18 inches) the waters rose above all the high mountains. And the ark was lifted up from the earth. And it moved on the face of the waters.

And the water covered the face of the earth five months, which is one hundred and fifty days. And all flesh was destroyed, BUT THE SPIRITS OF THE EVIL ONES WERE NOT DESTROYED. Having sought out the flesh of animals in which to live after their bodies were killed, THE SPIRITS OF THE GIANTS AND THE CHILDREN OF THE WATCHERS ESCAPED AND WAITED.

And the ark went and rested on the top of Lubar, one of the mountains of Ararat. On the new moon in the fourth month the fountains of the great deep were closed and the floodgates of heaven were restrained; and on the new moon of the seventh month all the mouths of the bottomless gulfs of the earth were opened, and the water began to flow down into the deep below. On the new moon of the tenth month the tops of the mountains were seen, and on the new moon of the first month the earth became visible. The waters disappeared from the earth in the fifth week in the seventh year of it, and on the seventeenth day in the second month the earth was dry.

On the twenty-seventh of it he opened the ark, and sent out beasts, and cattle, and birds, and every moving thing. AND THE SPIRITS OF THE EVIL ONES BEGAN TO INHABIT ANIMALS AND MEN ONCE AGAIN"

You can see from the text above that human beings and animals were re-inhabited after the flood. This accounts for the evil that we see in our day that can only be compared to the evil in the days of Noah.

10. **Nephilims (giants) are wiped out, but gibbors (tyrants and bullies) and sems (famous men) persist up till today.**

If the fallen angels were able to inhabit men and create monsters, they should still have the ability to do so. I see no reason why they would not want to continue invading human beings and destroying the human race. It is very likely that this practice is still on going.

However, giants do not find it easy to survive in a world of small-sized people. As you know, it is not easy to be of a large size and survive for very long. You are an easy target and become hated by everyone.

America is hated by many nations today because it is the one big super power that has everything. The sheer size of the giants and the dinosaurs is probably what led to their extinction. They were probably attacked and systematically eliminated and found it difficult to persist on earth. It is not easy for an over-sized creature to continue to exist in this world.

On the other hand, tyrants and famous men will find it easier to fit into the world. In history, there have been many notorious tyrants and famous men who have done deeds and exploits in our world.

Today, invading fallen angels are seen as famous men and tyrants, since they blend more into human society. It is most likely that many of the wicked, cruel and heartless tyrants we have experienced in our world were half demon / half human and that is why they had no human kindness or tenderness about them.

11. **Demons which are the spirits of the half-human, half-angel were released into the world upon the death of "nephilims" "gibbors" and "sems".**

The hybrid spirits of the three types of parahumans *gibbors* (tyrants and bullies), *sems* (famous men) and *nephilims* (giants)) are trapped in this world every time one of them dies. The spiritual part of these half human tyrants, giants and famous men continue to exist as unclean spirits. When these giant super-normal men-angels died, their half-human and half-angel spirits had to continue living on.

When a normal human being dies he either goes to heaven or hell to live eternally; but these para-humans are abnormalities which have to exist somewhere. Fallen angels continue to exist outside heaven's gates. Whenever a para-human dies, their spirits are confined to the earth and roam about as demons.

**And now, THE GIANTS, WHO ARE PRODUCED FROM THE SPIRITS AND FLESH, SHALL BE CALLED EVIL SPIRITS ON THE EARTH,**

**AND SHALL LIVE ON THE EARTH. Evil spirits have come out from their bodies because they are born from men and from the holy Watchers, their beginning is of primal origin;**

**THEY SHALL BE EVIL SPIRITS ON EARTH, and evil spirits shall they be called spirits of the evil ones.**

**Enoch 15:8-10**

Throughout the ministry of Jesus, He dealt with the devil and also with demons. But these are not one and the same thing.

Jesus dealt with two types of evil; *diabolos* and *diamonion*. In the Bible, the word "devil" is derived from the word *diabolos*, and the word "demon" is the word *diamonion*. *Diabolos* and *diamonion* are two different types of beings. However in the English language, we lump words together and use the words, "devil", "devils" "satan" and "demons" interchangeably.

So what are demons and what are they like? What do they look like and where do they come from? We know where satan, the fallen angels and the princes of darkness come from. So what are demons? Are they also fallen angels?

Demons are another set of creatures that Jesus dealt with called diamonion. These entities are not the same as fallen angels. According to the points we have gone through above, the demons were created by the death of the para-humans.

After the terrible invasion of human beings by fallen angels, the result was para-human and hybrid creatures, which become the evil spirits that we know as unclean spirits. This is the origin of the demons that inhabit our world. They are in the dark part of the world, and therefore they cannot be seen. The Book of Enoch is very clear on the fate of the fallen angels who inhabited human beings. It is also clear that the spiritual part of the giants, bullies and tyrants created by the combination of angels and human beings has continued to exist as evil spirits.

**And the angels which kept not their first estate, but left their own habitation, he hath reserved in everlasting chains under darkness unto the judgment of the great day.**

**Jude 1:6**

**And He answered and said to me, and I heard His voice: 'Do not be afraid, Enoch, you righteous man and scribe of righteousness.**

**Approach and hear my voice. Go and say to the Watchers of heaven, for whom you have come to intercede: "You should intercede for men, and not men for you."**

**Why and for what cause have you left the high, holy, and eternal heaven, and had sex with women, and defiled yourselves with the daughters of men and taken to yourselves wives, and done like the children of earth, and begotten giants (as your) sons?**

**Though you were holy, spiritual, living the eternal life, you have defiled yourselves with the blood of women, and have begotten children with the blood of flesh, and, as the children of men, you have lusted after flesh and blood like those who die and are killed.**

**This is why I have given men wives, that they might impregnate them, and have children by them, that**

deeds might continue on the earth.

But you were formerly spiritual, living the eternal life, and immortal for all generations of the world.

Therefore I have not appointed wives for you; you are spiritual beings of heaven, and in heaven was your dwelling place.

AND NOW, THE GIANTS, WHO ARE PRODUCED FROM THE SPIRITS AND FLESH, SHALL BE CALLED EVIL SPIRITS ON THE EARTH,

AND SHALL LIVE ON THE EARTH. EVIL SPIRITS HAVE COME OUT FROM THEIR BODIES BECAUSE THEY ARE BORN FROM MEN AND FROM THE HOLY WATCHERS, THEIR BEGINNING IS OF PRIMAL ORIGIN;

THEY SHALL BE EVIL SPIRITS ON EARTH, AND EVIL SPIRITS SHALL THEY BE CALLED SPIRITS OF THE EVIL ONES. [As for the spirits of heaven, in heaven shall be their dwelling, but as for the spirits of the earth which were born on the earth, on the earth shall be their dwelling.] And the spirits of the giants afflict, oppress, destroy, attack, war, destroy, and cause trouble on the earth.

They take no food, but do not hunger or thirst. They cause offences but are not observed.

And these spirits shall rise up against the children of men and against the women, because they have proceeded from them in the days of the slaughter and destruction.'

**Enoch 15:1-12**

And they began to sin against birds, and beasts, and reptiles, and fish, and to devour one another's flesh, and drank the blood. Then the earth laid accusation against the lawless ones.

**Enoch 7: 5-6**

There are several names that you are probably very familiar with. Hercules, Achilles, Cyclops and Medusa are some of the names we know very well. Few people realise that these were actually names of super-human and para-normal hybrid beings who once existed, according to Greek, Roman and Egyptian history.

There are indeed a number of stories that suggest Greeks had sex with animals. For instance, the story goes that a being called Zeus in the form of a bull, raped Europa and had three sons by her who founded the Cretan Culture.

Some people try to explain the stories of these monsters by saying that some still-born foetuses resemble monsters. Others also feel that the tales of these monsters result from a faulty observation of fossil bones. Whatever the case, these myths definitely do suggest that these types of unions did happen.

These super normal beings were so famous and notorious that their names are well known even in our modern times. I believe that these hybrid beings actually existed because their existence tallies with what we know from the book of Genesis and the Book of Enoch. We know that angels, who are non-human beings, had sex with humans and animals and created hybrid creatures that eventually died and became evil unclean spirits.

**And now, the giants, who are produced from the spirits and flesh, shall be called evil spirits on the earth,**

**And shall live on the earth. Evil spirits have come out from their bodies because they are born from men and from the holy watchers, their beginning is of primal origin;**

**they shall be evil spirits on earth, and evil spirits shall they be called spirits of the evil ones. [as for the spirits of heaven, in heaven shall be their dwelling, but as for the spirits of the earth which were born on the earth, on the earth shall be their dwelling.] And the spirits of the giants afflict, oppress, destroy, attack, war, destroy, and cause trouble on the earth.**

They take no food, but do not hunger or thirst. They cause offences but are not observed.

And these spirits shall rise up against the children of men and against the women, because they have proceeded from them in the days of the slaughter and destruction.'

**Enoch 15:8-12**

# CHAPTER 18

# Examples of Giants
# (Nephilim)

There were GIANTS (NEPHILIM) in the earth in those days; and also after that, when the sons of God came in unto the daughters of men, and they bare children to them, the same became mighty MEN (GIBBORIM) which were of old, MEN OF RENOWN (SEM)"

Genesis 6:4

Three different types of creatures were produced when angels interacted with human beings:

1. Giants

2. Famous men

3. Tyrants.

This chapter deals with the giants who once existed.

## GIANT SKELETONS CHART

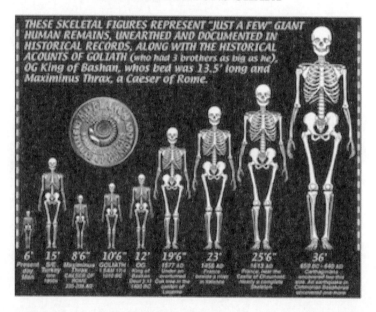

There have been several examples of *Sem* (famous men), *Gibbor* (bullies and tyrants) and *Nephilim* (giants) in human history. These men are not easily forgotten because they were unusual. Let us look at real life examples of (*Nephilim*) giants.

## 1.   A GIANT FINGER IN EGYPT

According to the German newspaper, BILD.de, a researcher named Gregor Spörri has presented a number of photos of a mummified giant finger. These incredible images are now being shown to the public for the first time. The finger is 15 inches long and if it is genuine, it belonged to someone who was more than 16 feet tall.

## A GIANT FINGER

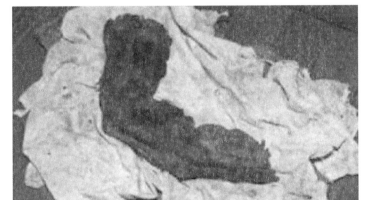

*Mummified giant finger. This photo[1] was taken during an excavation in 1988*

Could it also be that mega monuments such as some of the pyramids in Egypt, structures in Stonehenge, Easter Island, the Orcadian stones and others were constructed by an ancient race of giants? To our race as human beings, these stones appear incredibly massive, and they are. It is universally accepted that these massive stones and blocks require some type of mechanical advantage to handle and erect them. As large as these stones are, most seem to average about the same height everywhere they are found on Earth. These stones may not have been any much taller than any giants who may have mined, handled and erected them.

---

[1] Picture by Gregor Spörri

129

## 2.    A GIANT'S SKULL?

This is a greatly disputed picture of a skull purported to be the head of a giant. This "head of Goliath" is purported to have been discovered by a German archaeologist and made headlines in many newspapers.

## 3.    GIANTS IN IRAQ

In Sumerian (Iraqi) text and images, we see evidence of a giant race, such as depicted in the following tablet:

*Sumerian tablet with seated giant king*

How tall might this king be if he stood up? The more you study this image the more symbolism you'll find. Note the great detail in the king's attire and cuneiform writing in the clay.

## 4.   GIANTS IN SOUTH AMERICA

The first accounts of a race of giants living on the Pacific Coast of South America come from the chronicler on Ferdinand Magellan's voyage in 1520, Antonio Pigafetta.

Pigafetta tells of an entire race of the people who were said to be so tall that the tops of the Europeans' heads only reached to their waists. The captain, Magellan, named them "Patagonia" which came to mean "Land of the Bigfeet". Upon meeting the rest of the people, Magellan was said to be anxious to take a few of them back to Europe. They sent their strongest men to capture two, but the giants fell ill and died on the journey back to Europe.

Sir Francis Drake's nephew, in his published account of their journeys, told of their encountering massive giants. The voyage of John Byron of the British Royal Navy in the mid-1700s also seemed to confirm the tales. A book published two years after the ship's return told more stories about the giants.

## 5.   GIANTS IN WALES

There is an ancient copper mine near the coastal town of Llandudno in North Wales. This area rises 220 meters above the Irish Sea, and it is known as the location of the Great Orme

Copper Mine. It dates to the Bronze Age, about 3500 years ago. More than 2500 hammers have been recovered at the mine.

It is believed that the mine stretches for many kilometers, with six kilometers already surveyed. It is known to have nine levels within it, and over 1700 tons of copper are known to have been removed from the mine. This is quite a staggering accomplishment for a society of that era without the use of power tools, or at least as we know power tools today.

The largest typical sledgehammer used today weighs 20 pounds, though sledgehammers in the 10 pound class are more commonplace. A grown man (without back trouble yet) can wield a 20-pound hammer, but only for limited amounts of time.

An even bigger 64-pound sledgehammer was found at the copper mine by archeologists. To lift this 60 pound hammer using only the far end of a 9 foot long handle would be beyond the strength of any man. To swing it with force would be virtually impossible.

So who or what could have wielded one of these? If we scale the size of the ancient people so they could use this tool, the giants at the copper mine may have been perhaps 12 to 18 feet tall, or about 3 times taller than an average human being of today. To put this in perspective, the height of the wall in an average home in the United States built within the last 50 years in any given room is just 8 feet. Perhaps these are the people referred to in the Bible, in Genesis, where it says there were giants on the Earth in those days.

## 6. GIANTS IN GREEK HISTORY

### Cyclops

A cyclop, according to Greek and Roman history, was a member of a race of giants, each with a single eye in the middle of his forehead.

# CHAPTER 19

# Examples of Famous Men (Sem)

There were GIANTS (NEPHILIM) in the earth in those days; and also after that, when the sons of God came in unto the daughters of men, and they bare children to them, the same became mighty MEN (GIBBOR) which were of old, MEN OF RENOWN (SEM).

**Genesis 6:4**

# Examples of Sem (Famous Men)

Three different types of creatures were produced when angels interacted with human beings:

1. Giants

2. Famous Men and

3. Tyrants

This chapter deals with the famous men (*Sem*) who once existed.

There are many examples of famous men (*Sem*). Not all famous people are hybrids or para-human, but some are. The *Sem* are probably the largest group of para-humans existing on earth today. The *Nephilim* (giants) used to dominate the world and are mentioned very often in the Bible. Indeed, the children of Israel were afraid to enter the Promised Land because of these very giants. Giants, (large sized humans), no longer exist for the same reason that dinosaurs (large sized animals) no longer exist. *Nephilim* (giants) have been wiped out.

Bullies and tyrants, though still in existence, are greatly limited by the rise of democracy in our world today. Currently, there is a general intolerance of bullies and tyrants in our world. Bullies and tyrants are more likely to thrive in parts of the world where democracy is not strong or real.

In our world today, there are many people who become famous and notorious for various reasons. **There are many things that make people famous. Sometimes, people acquire fame because they are super-human and do things which are unusual and out of human character.** People who are hybrids between humans and angels develop unusual capabilities and often hold records in particular fields. There are others who are famous because of their inventions. Others are also famous for achievements in sports, wealth, television, inventions, music they produced, books they wrote and acting.

1. **There are people who are famous because of their murders.**

   There is a man who was said to abduct women and take them out to the Alaska wilderness. He would then strip them, let them go and hunt them down like animals, finally killing them with his hunting knife or his game rifle. He confessed to killing 17 women and raping 30 other women over a period of ten years.

   There is another man who is famous for taking an airliner and crashing it into the mountains, killing all one hundred and fifty passengers on board. Before he did this, he told his girlfriend that he would one day do something that would make him famous.

2. **There are people who are famous for their evil books and evil influence.**

   There are men who wrote books that promoted a kind of reasoning that turned millions away from God and ridiculed Christianity. One such man died in shame and had only six people attending his funeral because of the outrage that he caused with his notorious book that turned multitudes away from God.

3. **There are people who are famous for introducing the evil of pornography into the world.**

   There are people that are famous for their pornographic houses, pornographic films and pornographic performances.

4. **There are people who are famous for setting sexual records.**

   An American porn actress is reputed to have had sex with 919 men within 24 hours. She achieved this record in 2004 in Warsaw, Poland. It is said to be a feat that probably no other woman will ever accomplish.

During a ten-hour period in January 1995, another lady, a daughter of a middle-class Chinese couple, had sex with 251 men in front of cameras. The resulting video sold more than 40,000 copies. Unfortunately, she was never paid the agreed fee of $10,000. A documentary was made that tells the story about that day and her life as a student.

5. **There are people who are famous for their evil theories.**

The theory of evolution with secular, anti-Christian beliefs are famous in their power to turn people away from God over the centuries.

6. **There are people who are famous for their deception and treachery.**

Judas Iscariot is famous for betraying the Lord Jesus Christ. His treachery towards his master is world famous! There are people who are famous for selling secrets of their government, betraying entire civilizations and exposing the world to nuclear war.

7. **There are people who are famous for their evil music.**

Some musicians have sold millions of albums, charging the masses with spirits of lust, confusion, madness and drug abuse.

8. **There are people who are famous for their nakedness.**

One important queen is famous for riding naked on horseback through the city in order to convince her husband to lower taxes. The king issued an instruction that no one was to view his wife as she passed by. This instruction was disobeyed by a man called Tom who viewed the king's wife through his curtains. This incident gave rise to the name "Peeping Tom".

9. **There are people who are famous for the evil revolutions they started.**

One of the leaders of the French Revolution successfully argued for the execution of the king and continued to encourage crowds to rise up against the aristocracy. Another of the leaders of the French Revolution also encouraged the execution of enemies by the guillotine without trials. About 40,000 were either executed or died in prison including King Louis XVI and Queen Marie Antoinette.

10. **There are people who are famous for stirring up persecution of Jews.**

There are people who are famous for starting a tribunal to root out people they considered as threats to the Catholic Church. About twenty thousand Jews suffered death by being burned on stakes and other gruesome punishments.

# CHAPTER 20

# Examples of Tyrants and Bullies (Gibbor)

There were GIANTS (NEPHILIM) in the earth in those days; and also after that, when the sons of God came in unto the daughters of men, and they bare children to them, the same became mighty MEN (GIBBOR) which were of old, MEN OF RENOWN (SEM).

Genesis 6:4

Three different types of creatures were produced when angels interacted with human beings:

1. Giants;

2. Famous Men; and

3. Tyrants.

This chapter deals with the tyrants and bullies.

There have been many tyrants and bullies who have lived through the centuries. Many of these people were either possessed with devils or were simply the *Gibbor*. The *Gibbor* were a type of creature that was produced as a result of the combination of angels and human beings. If they were *Gibbor*, it means they were half human and half supernatural.

The crimes against humanity, the brutality, the wickedness and the lack of compassion, all reveal paranormal behaviour coming from super para-humans created by a combination of fallen angels and human beings.

Indeed, it is possible that many of these bullies and tyrants were not really "people". When they had unbridled power, they mutilated, murdered, tortured and tormented any one they wanted to.

Some of these people were super-human hybrids, simply a mixture of fallen angels and human beings. This is probably the only explanation for the inhumanness and the complete absence of feelings that some of these bullies and tyrants exhibited.

Below, I am presenting just a few of the tyrants and bullies that our world has endured. I have so many examples of bullies and tyrants, but for certain reasons, I have left out most of them.

This list is just a sample of a few bullies and tyrants. Some of these bullies and tyrants may have been super human hybrids. I can assure you that there are millions of people who are inhumanly wicked. There are many people from history who have lived as super human bullies and tyrants. There are also many people in our present world who clearly show signs of being para-normal. Perhaps, many of these wicked tyrants and bullies are actually the "*Gibbor*". It is very possible that some of them are superhuman combinations of fallen angels with human beings. As you read a little about them, you can decide for yourself whether they were normal human beings with normal feelings and compassion, or if they were superhuman. Read the accounts of each person that I have culled from historical accounts and educate yourself on a few of the types of human beings that have lived in our world. Today, Christians not only have to deal with people that are oppressed with the devil and possessed with evil spirits but also with people that are half-devil and half-human!

*Please note that I am not saying that the following people were half devil and half human.* I am saying that it is a possibility that they were half-devil and half-human. It is best for you to judge for yourself and decide whether you think they were half devil and half human or not.

## 1. Gaius Julius Caesar Augustus Germanicus (12 - 41 AD) (Caligula)

Caligula was a Roman Emperor who ruled for four years. He is remembered for the most awesomely disgusting, insane and luridly depraved crimes against humanity and morality.

He began by ordering the murders of anyone who had ever crossed him, or even disagreed with him on mundane matters. He had a very good memory. He exiled his own wife, and proclaimed himself a god, dressing up as Apollo, Venus (a goddess), Mercury and Hercules. He demanded that everyone, from senators to guards to guests and public crowds, refer to him as "divine" in his presence.

He attempted to appoint his favourite horse, Incitatus as a priest and consul, and ordered a beautiful marble stable built for him, complete with chairs and couches on which Incitatus never sat.

Once, at the Circus Maximus, the games ran out of criminals who were used to entertain the crowd by fighting with animals. The next event was the lions, his favorite. He then ordered his guards to drag the first five rows of spectators into the arena, which they did. These people were all devoured for his amusement.

A citizen once insulted him to his face in a fit of rage, and Caligula responded by having him tied down, and beaten with heavy chains. He made this last for 3 months, having the man brought out from a dungeon and beaten, until Caligula and the crowds that gathered were too offended by the smell of the man's gangrenous brain, whereupon he was beheaded.

Another man who insulted him had his entire family, publicly executed one after another in front of a crowd. The man and wife were first, followed by the oldest child and so on. The crowd became outraged and began to disperse, but many stayed to watch. The last of the family was a 12 year old girl, who was sobbing hysterically at what she had been forced to watch. A member of the crowd shouted that she was exempt from execution as a virgin. Caligula smiled and ordered the executioner to rape her and then strangle her, which he did.

Caligula's favourite torture was sawing. The saw blade filleted the spine and spinal cord from the chest down to the crotch. He also relished chewing up the testicles of victims, without biting them off, while they were restrained upside down before him.

He publicly had sex with his three sisters at banquets and games, sometimes on the table amid the food. He was finally murdered by the Praetorian Guard and some senators when he left the Circus Maximus after the games. His body was left in the street to rot, and dogs finally ate it.

Was this man a normal human being? Did he have any normal feelings of compassion? Could Caligula have been one of the bullies and tyrants the Bible describes as the "*Gibbor*"?

## 2.     Emperor Nero (54 – 68 AD)

There was a Roman Emperor who ruled from 54 - 68 AD. He systematically murdered every member in his family. He poisoned, beheaded, stabbed, burned, boiled, crucified and impaled thousands of people. He often raped women and also cut off the veins and private parts of both men and women.

He is said to have kicked one of his wives to death. He ordered his mother to be stabbed and clubbed to death. He was a strange mix of paradoxes; artistic, sporting, brutal, weak, sensual, erratic, extravagant, sadistic and bisexual.

This man did not want to be blamed for the burning of Rome and charged Christians for that. Because of this, Christians were covered with the skins of wild beasts, and torn by dogs. Other Christians were crucified. Others were set on fire, that they might serve for lights in the nighttime.

Sometimes Christians were covered with wax and other combustible materials, after which a sharp stake was put under their chin, to make them stand upright, and they were burnt alive, to give light to the spectators.

Was this bully a normal human being or was he a Gibbor? Was he possessed with devils! Was Emperor Nero half-human and half-demon?

## 3.     Ivan the Terrible (1530-1584)

Ivan was a man who ruled Russia in the sixteenth century. He was the first ruler of Russia to assume the title of Tsar.

In 1570, Ivan was under the belief that the elite of the city of Novgorod planned to defect to Poland, and led an army to stop them, on January 2. Ivan's soldiers built walls around the perimeter of the city in order to prevent the people of the city escaping. Between 500 and 1000 people were gathered every day by the troops, then tortured and killed in front of Ivan and his son.

In 1581, Ivan beat his pregnant daughter-in-law for wearing immodest clothing, causing a miscarriage. His son, also named Ivan, upon learning of this, engaged in a heated argument with his father, which resulted in Ivan striking his son in the head with his pointed staff, causing his son's (accidental) death.

Ivan the Terrible had his own personal torture chamber. He forced hundreds of parents to watch their children tortured and killed. He made bears and wolves eat hundreds of people.

He personally killed and tortured people with his long and hard staff. He gave orders for people to be beheaded, strangled, hanged, blinded, burned, stabbed, boiled, disembowelled, buried alive, impaled and fried. He often watched the executions, some of which were as long as 15 hours.

Was this man a normal human being? Did he have any human compassion? Why was he so wicked? Did he not have feelings as normal human beings do? Was he actually a super human tyrant?

## 4.    Emperor Commodus(161-192 AD)

Commodus was a Roman Emperor who ruled from 180 - 192 AD. His brutal rule led to civil strife that ended 84 years of stability and prosperity within that country.

He started performing as a gladiator and slaughtering many people. He adored the gladiatorial games, so much so that he personally entered many of them and fought alongside the gladiators, who were all criminals and slaves, etc. This severely offended the entire Empire, especially the Senate. The fighters who came into the arena with him just had wooden weapons, whilst he was well armed. He slaughtered many people in a bid to display manliness.

When his expensive lifestyle nearly made the imperial treasury bankrupt, he replenished it by accusing his senators of treason and having their property seized.

Commodus once ordered all the cripples, hunchbacks, and generally undesirables in the city to be rounded up, thrown into the arena, and forced to hack one another to death with meat cleavers.

He especially enjoyed killing animals, and killed 100 lions in one day, to the spectators' disgust. In addition to the crippled, Commodus would slay exotic animals, such as lions, ostriches, hippos, elephants, and giraffes. He killed three elephants singlehandedly in the arena, beheaded an ostrich and laughed at the senators attending, brandishing the head and motioning that they were next. He speared a giraffe to death, an animal which the spectators did not see as fearsome at all.

While fighting in the arena, opponents would submit to Commodus, as Emperor, and their lives were spared. However, in private practice fights, Commodus would slay his opponents. The Romans were outraged when Commodus would order wounded soldiers and amputees into the arena to be slayed. Non-military citizens who had lost their feet due to injury or illness would be tied together for Commodus to club to death. This horrified the Roman people.

The senators conspired to have him killed, and poisoned him, but he threw it up. They then sent in his favourite wrestler, a gladiator named Narcissus, who strangled him in his bath. His reign lasted 12 years, from 180 - 192 AD.

Was this man a normal person or was he superhuman?

## 5.    The American Cannibal

There was an American killer and cannibal. He was known for rape, murder and dismemberment of his victims. He murdered at least 17 men and boys over a period of thirteen years.

He raped his victims and often dismembered them before killing them. Sometimes, he even ate parts of his victims. He put some of the corpses of his victims in acid-filled vats in his apartment. He severed the heads of his victims and put them in his refrigerator. He was said to preserve all of parts of the corpses of those he killed. In fact, some skulls were found in his closet.

Was this a normal man or a *Gibbor*?

## 6.    The Grave Looter

A certain man who lived in America in the 1900s was known for outrageous acts. He was a killer and was found guilty of the murder of many women. He would also rob graves and keep body parts. He even made bowls out of human skulls and upholstered chairs with human flesh. He also made a belt made out of human nipples. He killed people, he scattered their body parts all around the town.

He used to live with his brother and mother and was very devoted to his mother.    When she died, he started visiting cemeteries to unearth newly buried females.    He would cut off some parts of the corpses as trophies and return the rest of the corpse to their graves.

Could this have been a normal man or was this a *Gibbor*?

## 7.    The Ejaculating Murderer

There was a certain man who became famous in his city for the wrong reasons. He murdered 53 women and children. In the seventies he lured a nine-year-old girl to an old house and attempted to rape her. When the girl struggled, he stabbed her to death. He ejaculated in the process of knifing the child to death.

From then on, he achieved sexual arousal and orgasm through stabbing and slashing women and children to death.

Was he a normal man or was he a *Gibbor*?    Why did he ejaculate whilst killing a child?    Are these normal feelings to expect from human beings?

## 8.    The Murdering Wife and Mother

In the nineteenth century there was a woman who lived in England.    She killed three of her four husbands to collect on their insurance policies. She also killed eleven of her fourteen children. She used arsenic poisoning to kill them, causing severe gastric pain to her victims.

This woman lacked human kindness and love that is expected towards a husband and children. Was she a normal woman or are we dealing with something more sinister?

## 9.    The Clown

There was a American man who was both a serial murderer and a clown. He first assaulted two teenage boys sexually and sentenced to 10 years in jail. After he was released on parole for excellent behaviour he proceeded to kill 33 young men. He then buried their bodies in his yard, in his house, or in the river near his house.

Because he was a clown, no one thought he was capable of such wickedness. What kind of person kills 33 people and buries them in his house? Was this wicked clown a normal human being or was there something more sinister about him?

## 10.    The Werewolf

There was an American man who was known as the "Werewolf". He was a man who molested over 100 children and more than five adults. He whipped his victims till they bled, cut up parts of their body, drank their blood and also ate parts of their bodies. He even sometimes roasted parts of the bodies and made stew with them, which he ate.

He had sexual obsessions, including coprophilia, urophilia, paedophilia and masochism. He even inserted needles in his own pelvis for sexual pleasure.

Was this apparently harmless looking man a *Gibbor*?

## 11.    The Acid Bath Murderer

The Acid Bath Murderer was an European who killed people and dissolved their bodies in acid. He lured his victims to a place, killed them and then dissolved their bodies in sulphuric acid.

One day, he had a sudden need for blood. So he hit his employer in the head with a blunt instrument, slit the man's throat, got a mug, took some of his employer's blood from his neck and drank it. He then dumped the body in a barrel, which he filled with sulphuric acid.

He even forged papers in order to sell the possessions of his victims and made substantial sums of money from those he had murdered. Was he a normal man or was he a *Gibbor*?

## 12.    The Asian Charmer

There was an Asian who killed as many as one hundred boys during an 18-month period.

He found the boys on the street and charmed them into his confidence. He then drugged them, raped them and strangled them. After he killed them, he cut up their bodies into pieces and put them in a vat filled with hydrochloric acid. Once all of the remains were liquefied, he then dumped the remains into the sewer.

Did this man have normal human feelings? Did this man act like a normal human being?

## 13.    The Female Guard

There was a lady who was a guard at a concentration camp during a War. Her hobby was collecting lampshades, book covers and gloves made from the skins of specially murdered concentration camp prisoners. She had a lady's handbag made out of the same material.

She continually tortured and killed so many people at the concentration camps that she was referred to as "the camp murderess". She would specially select prisoners with distinctive tattoos and these prisoners would be killed and their skin tanned.

She exploited her sexual appeal by parading around the camps on a horse, with a whip, and if any man so much as glanced at her she would have them whipped and shot on the spot.

Was this a normal woman? Where was the kindness that we expect from a woman and a mother? She was a bully and a tyrant in the concentration camps! Was she also a Gibbor?

## 14. The African Butcher

There was an African tyrant who did more than to murder those he considered his enemies. He subjected his victims to intense barbaric acts, even after they were dead. Several of the dead bodies of his victims that were dumped in the mortuary were terribly mutilated, with livers, noses, lips, genitals or eyes missing. Some would have both legs and arms amputated with the legs sewn where the arms should have been and the arms also put in place of the legs. When giving an instruction to murder someone, this tyrant would say, "Give him the VIP treatment" which meant, "torture him before you kill him."

This African butcher ordered killings of high-ranking officers whom he considered to be his opponents. He also ordered mass killings of members of the police, prisons and other civilians. Did this man have normal human feelings? Did this man act like a normal human being? Was he super human?

## 15. The African Cannibal

There was an African head of state who came to power through a coup d'etat. He ruled with an iron fist, torturing and killing political rivals and cutting off the ears of thieves.

Accusations of cannibalism were widespread. These accusations were triggered by photographs released in an European magazine that apparently showed a fridge containing the bodies of schoolchildren. It was also claimed his political rivals were cooked and served to visiting foreign dignitaries or fed to lions and crocodiles in his personal zoo. At his lavish coronation he spent millions of dollars to exalt himself as an emperor.

Did this man have normal human feelings? Did this man act like a normal human being? Was he super-human?

# CHAPTER 21

# How to Block the Activity of Devils Through Para-Humans

There were giants in the earth in those days; and also after that, when the sons of God came in unto the daughters of men, and they bare children to them, the same became mighty men which were of old, men of renown.

**Genesis 6:4**

**P**ara-humans are a great threat to God's people in whatever way they manifest. You must watch out for them and overcome the danger they pose by using the wisdom of God. You have to deal with para-humans with the wisdom of God. Sometimes you have to deal with para-human activity by avoiding them. Sometimes civilization, development and democracy are things that have limited the power of para-humans and super-humans in this world. Sometimes, it is a well developed army, police and a good government that deal with para-human activity on earth. If there were no civilization, democracy or police, bullies and tyrants would roam the streets and terrorise ordinary people. Para-humans would spread their fear and influence everything, if left unchecked.

## 1. Block the activity of para-humans that are giants.

Giants were a real threat in the olden days when size meant power. Giants were a great threat to God's people all through the Bible. There were many threats from giants against God's people in Bible times. Some of the famous giants were people like Goliath who threatened David's life and ministry. There were other giants in the land of Canaan who threatened the life and ministry of Moses, Joshua and Caleb.

> **And there went out a champion out of the camp of the Philistines, named Goliath, of Gath, WHOSE HEIGHT WAS SIX CUBITS AND A SPAN.**
>
> **1 Samuel 17:4**

The story of David and Goliath is a story about real people who were threatened by super human giants. Goliath threatened to wipe out God's people because of his super human size.

Joshua and Caleb's team of spies were also threatened by giants in the land of Canaan.

> **And they brought up an evil report of the land which they had searched unto the children of Israel, saying, The land, through which we have gone to search it, is a land that eateth up the inhabitants thereof; and all the**

people that we saw in it are men of a great stature. And there WE SAW THE GIANTS, the sons of Anak, which come of the giants: and we were in our own sight as grasshoppers, and so we were in their sight.

Numbers 13:32-33

David and his mighty men had to fight other giants, including the brother of Goliath.

And there was war again with the Philistines; and Elhanan the son of Jair slew LAHMI THE BROTHER OF GOLIATH the Gittite, whose spear staff was like a weaver's beam.

And yet again there was war at Gath, where was a man of great stature, whose fingers and toes were four and twenty, six on each hand, and six on each foot: and HE ALSO WAS THE SON OF THE GIANT. But when he defied Israel, Jonathan the son of Shimea David's brother slew him.

1 Chronicles 20:5-7

Fortunately, in our time the large sizes of both animals and humans have already been wiped out. It is not easy for oversized human beings or animals to continue to thrive as their large size paradoxically makes them more vulnerable.

2.   **Block the activity of para-humans that come with unusual strength.**

When Jesus got out of the boat, a man with an evil spirit came from the tombs to meet him. This man lived in the tombs, and NO ONE COULD BIND HIM any more, NOT EVEN WITH A CHAIN. For he had often been chained hand and foot, but he tore the chains apart and broke the irons on his feet. NO ONE WAS STRONG ENOUGH TO SUBDUE HIM.

Mark 5:2-4 (NIV)

Anybody with super-human strength can be a threat. The mad man of Gadara was a threat to the people around because no one could control him. Strong men have often posed a threat to the rest of their community by becoming bullies and tyrants.

Fortunately today, you cannot easily threaten people because of your unusual strength. Super human strength is easily neutralised by modern technology. Modern weapons like guns, bombs and grenades neutralise the super-human strength of fighters and bullies. There are many films about fighters and bullies which we all enjoy watching. Fighters and bullies are of great interest to the human race because of their great power. Once again, wisdom from God has nullified the powers of para-humans endowed with unusual strength.

3. **Block the activity of para-humans with superhuman wickedness.**

**Without natural affection, trucebreakers, false accusers, incontinent, fierce, despisers of those that are good,**

**2 Timothy 3:3**

There are people who are well known to be very wicked. History has experienced the wickedness of tyrants like Nero, Caligula, Hitler and Atilla the Hun. Their wickedness is legendary. When such people have power, their evil is unleashed on people.

Such people are a threat to their world. When men without compassion exercise their superhuman wickedness on the population, it is not easy to even exist in the country.

People who lack compassion are a threat to society. When these people are in power, they unleash their lack of compassion on the people. There should be some amount of pity in the heart of a person. That pity would usually limit the manifestations of wickedness.

Fortunately, the wisdom of democracy wipes out the power of people with super human wickedness. A good and effective police force and military also limits the powers of people who lack compassion. Good Christians must fight demons by supporting the presence of a good police service and a good government. Sometimes you may have to leave a country to avoid the bullies and tyrants who have come into power.

**4. Block the activity of para-human sexual desires.**

**Therefore God gave them over in the sinful desires of their hearts TO SEXUAL IMPURITY for the degrading of their bodies with one another.**

**Romans 1:24 (NIV)**

Para-human sexual desires refer to when people do not have a natural desire any more. You must prevent yourself from developing para-normal sexual desires. Some para-humans are super sex machines. Such people have abnormal quantities of abnormal sex. There are people who go around with great desires to have sex all the time. Many have fallen victim to such sexual predators. Some people even marry people with such desires for abnormal sex.

**Because of this, God gave them over to shameful lusts. Even their women exchanged natural relations for unnatural ones. In the same way the MEN ALSO ABANDONED NATURAL RELATIONS WITH WOMEN and were inflamed with lust for one another. Men committed indecent acts with other men, and received in themselves the due penalty for their perversion.**

**Furthermore, since they did not think it worthwhile to retain the knowledge of God, he gave them over to a depraved mind, to do what ought not to be done.**

**Romans 1:26-28 (NIV)**

As mentioned earlier, para-human sexual desires refer to when people do not have a natural desire any more. In the scripture above, men have a desire for other men instead of having a desire for women. Some human beings have abandoned natural relations and adopted para-normal sexual desires as their norm. Some have abandoned natural relations and given themselves to sexually desire after animals. Some have abandoned the natural relations for adults and adopted para-normal sexual desires for children.

As evil spirits take over human beings, they begin to call these para-human desires "human rights". Today, people are fighting for the right to marry animals.

As evil spirits dominate human beings, they call the reading of our ancient scriptures "hate speech". These evil spirits seek to dominate human society until super-human and para-human behaviour is accepted as normal. It is indeed the invasion of human beings by evil spirits that creates gross abnormalities in human behaviour.

By the reading of the scriptures and by standing firmly by what the Word of God says, the onslaught of para-human sexual desires will neither affect you nor influence you.

# CHAPTER 22

# How to Overcome Animal-like Demons

And he asked him, WHAT IS THY NAME? And he answered, saying, my name is Legion: for we are many.

**Mark 5:9**

Jesus taught us how to deal with the devil! The master key to dealing with the enemy is to find out whom you are dealing with. This is why Jesus asked the most famous and the most important of all questions in the field of demonology: "What is your name?"

What is your name? Who am I talking to? What am I dealing with? Who exactly are you? Where do you hail from? Where do you come from? I want to fight you, crush you, expel you and dispense with you!

## Why Jesus Asked the Devil, "What is Your Name?"

A basic principle of war is to know your enemy and know a lot about him. The way to fight your enemy is to know his name and to know as much as possible about him.

This is why Jesus asked the question, "What is your name?"

In other words, "Whom am I talking to? Whom am I dealing with?"

Know your enemy and know yourself! The more you know about your enemy, the more likely you are to win in a fight against him. How can you shoot somebody down if you do not know what he looks like? You must know his name, which will tell you a lot about his size, his location and his movements.

I want you to make every effort to know your enemy - to know where he lives, to know what he looks like, to know what he does, to know what he has and to understand him. I want you to know how the enemy was created and know what exactly he is doing in our world.

This is what Moses did when he sent out the spies into the Promised Land. He was making special efforts to know about his enemy. Moses did not want to fight a war with someone he did not know a lot about.

**And MOSES SENT THEM TO SPY OUT THE LAND of Canaan, and said unto them, Get you up this way southward, and go up into the mountain:**

**And SEE THE LAND, WHAT IT IS; AND THE PEOPLE THAT DWELLETH THEREIN, WHETHER THEY BE STRONG OR WEAK, FEW OR MANY;**

**And what the land is that they dwell in, whether it be good or bad; and what cities they be that they dwell in, whether in tents, or in strong holds;**

**And what the land is, whether it be fat or lean, whether there be wood therein, or not. And be ye of good courage, and bring of the fruit of the land. Now the time was the time of the firstripe grapes.**

**Numbers 13:17-20**

Someone said, "Know your enemy and know yourself and in a hundred battles you will never be in danger." This book will give you more details about the enemy. This book will help you understand and defeat the evil creatures you are fighting in the spirit world.

When you know what you are fighting with, you can call them out by name and bind them. Demons respond a hundred times better when you call them out by name. Anyone would jump when you shout out his name! You will notice how your heart starts to beat when you hear your name being called out.

This is exactly what happens to the devil when he hears his exact name being called out. This is why God gives visions and dreams. He gives visions to unveil the wicked spirits that are behind the struggles and difficulties of your life and ministry. When you see what is behind the veil, you can attack it. You can call it out by name and curse it, rebuke it and command fire to fall on it.

**By faith he forsook Egypt, not fearing the wrath of the king: for he endured AS SEEING HIM WHO IS INVISIBLE.**

**Hebrews 11:27**

It is time to grow up and see the spirit world. Moses did well because he saw the invisible world and acted accordingly. To be a Christian is to walk by faith. To be a Christian is to see the invisible. Can you see the invisible? Do you believe what you read in the Bible? Do you believe the creatures described in the Bible are real? It is time to see the invisible and walk by faith. That is the only way you can have a good report. Many of us do not understand how the dark world of evil spirits came about. What are evil spirits and where did they come from?

There are different types of evil spirits. Some evil spirits are fallen angels. Some evil spirits are para-humans. Some evil spirits are deities or devils. Even within the dark world, there are classes of evil spirits.

You must make special efforts to understand the enemy spirits we are at war with. Who are they? What do they look like? Where do they come from? Where do they live? How do they affect us? What do they do to us? Do they have power over us or do we have power over them?

Make special efforts to read and to study all you can about these evil spirits. I once spoke to the principal of a Bible school and asked him which books they use in the study of demonology. He answered, "There are no demons in this school! There is nothing like demonology in our curriculum!" I almost felt stupid for asking a question about demonology.

You must know about all kinds of evil creatures including fallen angels, devils and para-humans because you are living in the midst of them. The whole world lies in wickedness. The wickedness of our world is controlled by many types of evil spirits that have been in existence long before we came on the scene. It is an over-simplification to say that we are dealing with one senior evil spirit called satan and a thousand other junior evil spirits called demons. We are dealing with much more than that. We are dealing with many different types of entities, beings, creatures and powers.

The whole world truly lieth in wickedness and satan is the god of this world. Today, violence, wickedness and immorality are multiplying all around us. You and I are operating in a world that lies under the control of many evil powers.

**And we know that we are of God, and the whole world lieth in wickedness.**

**1 John 5:19**

To be victorious, you must know and understand the world in which you have found yourself and you must become successful at dealing with these unseen but very real enemies.

Apostle Paul made mention of different types of evil spirits that we have to deal with. Principalities, powers, rulers of the darkness and wicked spirits in high places are four well-known groups of evil spirits (Ephesians 6:12).

However, there are many other types of creatures and entities described in the Bible. There is a very dark world that is full of wickedness. It is this dark world that determines what happens in our physical world. If you read your Bible carefully, you will notice many different beings that are described or referred to. Even the briefest mention of an evil creature in the Bible deserves your attention. The mention of these creatures lets you know that they exist and they are at war with us.

**He that committeth sin is of the devil; for the devil sinneth from the beginning. For this purpose the Son of God was manifested, that he might destroy the works of the devil.**

**1 John 3:8**

As a servant of God you are to continue with the mission of Jesus. And the mission of Jesus is to destroy the works of the devil. How can you destroy the works of the devil when you do not know who he is and what he is like? How can you destroy the works of the devil when you do not know the different forms he takes? Indeed, there are many reasons why you must know a lot about evil spirits, evil powers and their operations. Today, there are Bible schools which proudly declare that they do not study about demons. "We have no demons in our school," they happily declare.

Dear friend, you are deceiving yourself if you think you will live this life without having to fight the various kinds of evil creatures that exist. Dealing with devils, demons, principalities, thrones, dragons, serpents, powers, entities, spiritual hybrids, para-humans, leviathan spirits, fallen angels is part of our Christianity.

## The animal spirits do what their physical counterparts do:

1.  **The spiritual forces that came for Elijah were used for chariots and transportation just as natural horses are used for transportation. The spiritual horses in the book of Revelation were used for horse-riding just as physical horses are used for horse-riding.**

    And it came to pass, as they still went on, and talked, that, behold, there appeared a chariot of fire, and horses of fire, and parted them both asunder; and Elijah went up by a whirlwind into heaven.

    And Elisha saw it, and he cried, my father, my father, the chariot of Israel, and the horsemen thereof. And he saw him no more: and he took hold of his own clothes, and rent them in two pieces.

    2 Kings 2:11-12

2.  **A serpent in the Bible deceived Eve. In the same way that natural serpents deceive people about their presence, their absence, their harmlessness, their concealment, their blending with the environment till someone steps on them accidentally.**

And the Lord God called unto Adam, and said unto him, Where art thou? And he said, I heard thy voice in the garden, and I was afraid, because I was naked; and I hid myself. And he said, who told thee that thou wast naked? Hast thou eaten of the tree, whereof I commanded thee that thou shouldest not eat? And the man said, the woman whom thou gavest to be with me, she gave me of the tree, and I did eat.

And the Lord God said unto the woman, what is this that thou hast done? And the woman said, THE SERPENT BEGUILED ME, and I did eat.

Genesis 3:9-13

3.    **The spiritual lion in the Bible goes about roaring just as the natural lion goes about roaring.**

Be sober, be vigilant; because your adversary the devil, as A ROARING LION, walketh about, seeking whom he may devour:

1 Peter 5:8

4.    **The spiritual birds are kept in a cage just as natural birds are kept in a cage.**

And he cried mightily with a strong voice, saying, Babylon the great is fallen, is fallen, and is become the habitation of devils, and the hold of every foul spirit, and A CAGE OF EVERY UNCLEAN AND HATEFUL BIRD.

Revelation 18:2

5.    **It stands to reason that the spiritual flies and insects will bring disease just as the natural ones do.**

And the Lord did so; and there came a grievous swarm of flies into the house of Pharaoh, and into his servants' houses, and into all the land of Egypt: THE LAND WAS CORRUPTED BY REASON OF THE SWARM OF FLIES.

Exodus 8:24

6.  **We accidentally step on natural scorpions and they sting us. In the same way, Jesus gives us power to tread upon scorpions.**

And he said unto them, I beheld Satan as lightning fall from heaven. Behold, I give unto you POWER TO TREAD ON serpents and SCORPIONS, and over all the power of the enemy: and nothing shall by any means hurt you.

Luke 10:18-19

## Ten Types of Animal-like Demons

1.  **Flies are launched against you from the spiritual realm:**

And the scribes which came down from Jerusalem said, He hath BEELZEBUB, and by the prince of the devils casteth he out devils.

And he called them unto him, and said unto them in parables, How can Satan cast out Satan? And if a kingdom be divided against itself, that kingdom cannot stand.

Mark 3:22-24

2.  **Hateful spiritual birds are launched against you from the spiritual realm:  Some demons are referred to as hateful birds.**

And he cried mightily with a strong voice, saying, Babylon the great is fallen, is fallen, and is become the habitation of devils, and the hold of every foul spirit, and a cage of EVERY UNCLEAN AND HATEFUL BIRD.

Revelation 18:2

3.  **Frog spirits are launched against you from the spiritual realm:  Some demons are referred to as frogs.**

And I saw three UNCLEAN SPIRITS LIKE FROGS come out of the mouth of the dragon, and out of the mouth

163

of the beast, and out of the mouth of the false prophet. For they are the spirits of devils, working miracles, which go forth unto the kings of the earth and of the whole world, to gather them to the battle of that great day of God Almighty.

Revelation 16:13-14

**4.    Scorpions are launched against you from the spiritual realm:  Some evil spirits are referred to as scorpions.**

Behold, I give unto you power to tread on serpents and SCORPIONS, and over all the power of the enemy: and nothing shall by any means hurt you.

Luke 10:19

**5.    Dragons are launched against you from the spiritual realm:  Some evil spirits are referred to as dragons.**

And THE GREAT DRAGON WAS CAST OUT, that old serpent, called the Devil, and Satan, which deceiveth the whole world: he was cast out into the earth, and his angels were cast out with him.

Revelation 12:9

**6.    Spiritual snakes are launched against you from the spiritual realm:  Some evil spirits are referred to as serpents.  Obviously, these are not physical snakes but spiritual snakes.**

And THE SERPENT cast out of his mouth water as a flood after the woman, that he might cause her to be carried away of the flood.

Revelation 12:15

**7.    Spiritual horses are launched against you from the spiritual realm:**

And I looked, and behold a pale horse: and his name that sat on him was Death, and Hell followed with him. And power was given unto them over the fourth part of the earth, to kill with sword, and with hunger, and with death, and with the beasts of the earth.

Revelation 6:8

**8.  A spiritual sea monster is launched against you from the spiritual realm:  Some evil spirits are referred to as Leviathan.  Leviathan is a well-known sea monster or sea creature with many heads.**

Thou brakest the heads of LEVIATHAN in pieces, and gavest him to be meat to the people inhabiting the wilderness.

Psalms 74:14

**9.  A multiple-headed monster in the sea is launched against you from the spiritual realm:  Some demons are multiple-headed monsters living in the sea.  Some call these marine spirits.**

And I stood upon the sand of the sea, and saw A BEAST RISE UP OUT OF THE SEA, having seven heads and ten horns, and upon his horns ten crowns, and upon his heads the name of blasphemy.

Revelation 13:1

**10.  A multiple-headed monster under the earth is launched against you from the spiritual realm:  Some demons are multiple-headed monsters in the earth. These are terrestrial spirits.**

And I beheld ANOTHER BEAST COMING UP OUT OF THE EARTH; and he had two horns like a lamb, and he spake as a dragon.

Revelation 13:11

## How to detect the presence of Animal-like Devils

The presence of animal-like demons is easy to detect by noticing animal symptoms in the nature of attacks that you experience.

1.  **Surprises, ambushes and traps such as sudden evil events speak of a serpent in action.** Serpents are well-known for their surprise attacks. You never see it coming. You never know where it is waiting. The suddenness of the attack shows you a snake spirit is present.

2.  **Attacks of the enemy that corrupt and contaminate speak of serpents.** The poison that destroys a church and takes away the sweetness that once existed comes from a snake. A human life is completely destroyed because of a drop of poison that changes everything. Watch out for things that contaminate your joy and your love. Watch out for things that spoil the church and change the good atmosphere of joy, peace and love. Watch out for those that bring about unhappiness, discontentment, murmuring and confusion. I believe they are carrying a serpent spirit that poisons and contaminates!

3.  **Attacks of the enemy against your life that are loaded with fear, terror and fright often mean a lion spirit is present.** There is no one who does not panic when he hears the roar of a lion nearby. I once watched a film based on a true story in which there were many sick people being nursed in a large hospital tent. Some of them were on drips and some of them were half conscious. At a point in the film, a lion entered the tent and roared. This was the fastest "miracle service" I ever saw. Every single patient rose from their deathbed and leaped out of the tent. The fear of the roaring lion galvanized every one into action. Lions, indeed, create real fear!

    Attacks of the enemy in which you are dealing with a proud and stubborn person could also mean that you are dealing with a lion spirit. Lions are known to stubbornly move forward and rarely ever retreat or change their minds. Watch out for pride and stubbornness. Cats are proud and a lion is a cat!

A lion which is strongest among beasts, and turneth not away for any;

Proverbs 30:30

4. **Attacks of the enemy, which involve sickness and disease often have to do with flies, insects and disease-spreading agents.** Indeed, the spirit versions of these insects and flies behave just like their physical counterparts and bring disease, illness and death to their victims. One of satan's well-known names is "lord of the flies". He is the commander of the disease agents.

5. **Attacks of the enemy that bring discomfort and unease could mean a frog spirit is present.**

And I saw three UNCLEAN SPIRITS LIKE FROGS come out of the mouth of the dragon, and out of the mouth of the beast, and out of the mouth of the false prophet. "For they are the spirits of devils, ...."

Revelation 16:13-14

Frogs are not destructive in themselves but they do make you feel uneasy. Their presence makes everything uncomfortable and unpalatable. There are many times your comfort is taken away, your ease is taken away and your rest is taken away by a demonic attack. This kind of demonic attack is most probably caused by a frog spirit. The effect of the frog spirit is to make you feel uneasy, nervous and anxious. Without peace, without comfort, and without restedness there are many things you cannot achieve.

# CHAPTER 23

# How You Can Stop Demons from Entering Your Body

**Neither give place to the devil.**

**Ephesians 4:27**

S atan enters into someone he has been seducing and is able to do a mighty evil work.

Then entered Satan into Judas surnamed Iscariot, being of the number of the twelve. And he went his way, and communed with the chief priests and captains, how he might betray him unto them.

Luke 22:3-4

Then goeth he, and taketh with himself seven other spirits more wicked than himself, and THEY ENTER IN and dwell there: and the last state of that man is worse than the first. Even so shall it be also unto this wicked generation.

Matthew 12:45

Do you enter a house from just anywhere? Do you not enter a house through its doors? If demons see you as a house, then you must have a door that the devils will target. Why are the devils interested in the doors of the house? Why are thieves interested in knowing where the doors of a house are? Because they are interested in gaining access to the house! Why do people strengthen the doors of their home? Why do people invest in security doors? Because it can be the point of entry of wicked and evil men!

If demons are to enter a body, they will have to do so through the entry points and doors. It is important for believers to know about these doors so that they do not become points of access to demons.

As a human being, you must be aware of the six openings in your body. Each of these holes leads to a deeper and inner section of your being. The human body has six main holes or portals of entry. Each of these can be an excellent and appropriate doorway to an evil spirit. You will notice that sinful activity in any of these holes leads to evil spirits entering human beings. You must guard these holes or doors carefully, because they are the doors that are targeted by evil spirits.

## 1.    THE DOOR OF THE EAR

The ear is the most important door through which imaginations of demons are launched into the mind. What you hear makes you think! Jesus warned us to be careful about what you allow yourself to hear.

**And he said unto them, TAKE HEED WHAT YE HEAR: with what measure ye mete, it shall be measured to you: and unto you that hear shall more be given.**

**Mark 4:24**

What you think about develops into an idea and into a complex imagination. By hearing the wrong things, satan's ideas and imaginations are launched into your mind. Once satan is able to capture your mind with depression, fear, lust and revenge, you come under his power. Adolf Hitler became anti-Semitic and a murderer of fifty million people by hearing common men on the street speak evil of Jews. He then gradually developed a hatred for Jews. Faith comes by hearing and hearing by the word of God. Imaginations also come by hearing. Thoughts and ideas come by hearing. Your ear is therefore a portal for the entry of demons. That is why Jesus taught us, "Take heed what you hear".

To understand how satan can gain entry into your life, you must learn from Adam and Eve. How did satan become involved in two perfect human beings who were having a good time together? Satan spoke to them and tried to get them to sin. As soon as they sinned and disobeyed God, satan was a part of their lives.

To sin is to yield to the devil. It is to say "yes" to the devil, making him a kind of boss or commander in your life. Once satan is a commander in your life, you are under him and under his management. As you can see, anyone or anything that is under the leadership of satan is doomed to sin, wickedness, harshness, despair, depression, sorrow, pain and continual darkness. You will not want to have satan as your master. Any kind of sin opens a door and gives more access to evil spirits.

Satan entered the lives of the human race by talking to Eve and making her imagine something wonderful, like being like God. Her imaginations got the better of her and she decided to yield to the pressure that came on her through the serpent. She thought that the things satan promised would happen. She thought she would have something nicer than she had already. But satan did not fulfil any of his promises. She, her husband and the entire human race were destroyed when she opened the door by listening with her ears to the devil's lies. You must be very careful about what you hear. Do not think that you are stronger or better than Eve. There are some things you should just not hear!

Quiet people are in greater danger of becoming demonized because they are often thinking instead of speaking. Instead of sharing their hearts, their problems and their lives with others, they think deeply and muse over many evil and dark thoughts. This is why the Bible teaches us to cast away imaginations.

**(For the weapons of our warfare are not carnal, but mighty through God to the pulling down of strong holds;) CASTING DOWN IMAGINATIONS, and every high thing that exalteth itself against the knowledge of God, and bringing into captivity every thought to the obedience of Christ;**

**2 Corinthians 10:4-5**

Imaginations are thoughts that are developing, growing and spreading. I am often uneasy in the presence of people who are unduly quiet. I can never tell what they are thinking about. Do they like me? Do they hate me? Do they think I am cheating them? Are they planning something? Recently, a pilot with dark and suicidal thoughts flew a plane full of passengers into the French Alps. When his computer was investigated, they found that he had researched several times on how to commit suicide! Such a person is full of dark thoughts but will not share what he is thinking. Every one on the plane was in danger of this man's dark thoughts. Indeed, every one on that flight perished because they did not know what he was thinking! It is dangerous to assume that a quiet person is thinking good thoughts! If you are a quiet, moody person, you must watch out because you are in danger of having malevolent evil spirits enter you, live in you and roam through your soul!

## 2.    THE DOOR OF THE EYE

**The light of the body is the eye: therefore when thine eye is single, thy whole body also is full of light; but WHEN THINE EYE IS EVIL, thy body also is full of darkness.**

**Luke 11:34**

The eye is a welcome door to demons that want to enter you. You must remember that many imaginations and thoughts are the power of the devil in action. That is why Paul taught us to cast down imaginations which exalt themselves above the knowledge of God (2 Corinthians10:5).

The eye is the portal through which visions, pictures and ideas enter the brain. This is why the Bible warns us about what we see. Many evil spirits flood into men as they watch pornography and other perversions. Abnormal desires, abnormal feelings and lusts constantly swell up in young men as they watch pornography for hours on end. Many people are never the same again after their lives are impacted by pornography.

Many people become violent murderers after watching certain films. People learn how to kill, fight and destroy by watching certain movies. The presence of these evil spirits completely changes their personalities and makes them go contrary to their love for God.

There are several cases of murder that are linked to young people watching films and learning how to do it. Through the eye, imaginations are launched into the mind and the power of the devil is established.

This is why you must protect yourself from seeing the wrong thing. You must also protect your children from watching films that bring about the spirit of fear in them. Some children are never the same after watching certain ghost films. Many girls are filled with the spirit of fear after watching certain films. Many people are filled with the spirit of love affairs and adultery after watching soap operas. You must watch out for your eyes! Give yourself to watching preaching DVDs and other spirit-filled movies. Anyone who spends several hours a day watching movies is likely to be affected by evil spirits.

## 3. THE DOOR OF THE MOUTH

Death is not just the stopping of your heartbeat. Death is a person! Death is a spirit! Death is a rider of a horse! It is the coming of a spirit into your life. It is the spirit of death. Satan is originally a murderer. This means that satan is first and foremost a killer or a taker away of life. Death comes to people through many of the foods that are eaten. In the verse below, you see how death is actually a rider on a horse.

**And I looked, and behold a pale horse: AND HIS NAME THAT SAT ON HIM WAS DEATH, and Hell followed with him. And power was given unto them over the fourth part of the earth, to kill with sword, and with hunger, and with death, and with the beasts of the earth.**

**Revelation 6:8**

The mouth is an important entry hole to your body. Many evil spirits and many diseases enter the body through the mouth. Many water-borne and water-related diseases come to the body through the mouth. Many diseases enter the body through food that is eaten. Salmonellosis, diarrhoea, cholera, dysentery and typhoid fever also enter the body through the mouth. The guinea worm infection comes into the body when you drink contaminated water.

Today, scientists have confirmed how fats, oil and many other foods we take in cause disease, sickness and death. Death is a person, a spirit and a rider who can come into your life through your mouth.

One of the important things you learn from Jesus is how He gave thanks before He ate. Many animals are possessed with evil spirits and many evils come into your body through the mouth. Praying over the food you eat is more than a ritual. It is sanctification and cleansing of what is about to enter you.

## 4.    THE DOOR OF THE NOSE

One of the greatest doors to evil spirits is the nose.

Many of the smallest but most deadly viruses come into human beings through the nose. Many worldwide epidemics which killed thousands of people came to the human body through the nose. The flu is caused by the influenza virus. As people sneeze and cough and breathe, they pass this virus to the next person who breathes it in. Some people do not travel on airplanes because they may breathe in a virus, bacteria or some kind of sickness that can kill them.

This is why very ill people are advised not to fly, because there are so many diseases they can get on board a flight where they are enclosed for several hours.

Did you notice how many people were killed by the Ebola virus and the bird flu virus? The spirit of death enters the human race through the nose. Science has shown us that it is viruses that are causing the diseases and deaths. Through the Bible, we know even more than what science can teach us.

When children are born, they are immediately vaccinated against tuberculosis, which is an airborne disease. Through medical science, we are able to block the spirit of death that wants to kill our new-born children.

Walk in wisdom by not inhaling evil into your life through your nose. Through the power and wisdom of science, you will block activities of murderous demons in your life.

## 5.    THE DOOR OF THE VAGINA

Your vagina is a favourite door for demons!  In every home there is a favourite door!  There may be three entrances to a house but everyone may end up passing through the kitchen door.  In the same way, there may be six doors to your body, but the vagina is truly a popular and favourite door for demons.

What is the vagina?  The vagina is an opening in a female body through which babies are born.  It is also the organ that is penetrated during sexual intercourse and during the sin of fornication.  Through sinful sexual intercourse (which takes place through the vagina), evil spirits enter into women.

You will notice that many women fall down under the power of God and manifest with screaming, rolling and crying.  Often, the vaginal door has been breached and evil spirits have entered these women.  Indeed, fornication is the only sin that is directly linked to the entrance and presence of evil spirits and creatures.  Notice this very clear scripture that tells us exactly how and why evil spirits entered into Babylon.

**And he cried mightily with a strong voice, saying, Babylon the great is fallen, is fallen, and is BECOME THE HABITATION OF DEVILS, and the hold of every foul spirit, and a cage of every unclean and hateful bird. FOR ALL NATIONS HAVE DRUNK OF THE WINE OF THE WRATH OF HER FORNICATION, and the kings of the earth have committed fornication with her, and the merchants of the earth are waxed rich through the abundance of her delicacies.**

**Revelation 18:2-3**

Why did Babylon become the habitation of devils?  Why do people become the habitation of devils?  Why would a woman become the habitation of devils?  As you can see from this scripture, many evil spirits and many entities occupied Babylon, simply because of her fornication.  This is a direct and clear statement that needs no interpretation or explanation.

When fornication is at a certain level, evil spirits of immorality flood the female body through the vagina and enter the woman making her a habitation. Such women, who are flooded by spirits of immorality, become even more sexually active, more sexually attractive and even more sexually inviting. This is why such women continue to fornicate with a longer and longer list of men. Demonised women are so sexually attractive that men are drawn to them like flies. Men are drawn to these women supernaturally because their attraction is supernatural and super-human. The demons inflate their beauty and their sexual appeal, so that the unsuspecting and the unspiritual cannot keep themselves away. Spiritual men are usually put off by such hyper-inflated beauties that seem to be nothing but a plate of sexual delights marching up and down in front of us.

The supernatural nature of this attraction can be seen when older and less attractive women with such spirits seem to continually and persistently draw men to themselves. Have you not noticed many old and unattractive prostitutes who inexplicably draw hundreds of clients to themselves?

It is not only the spirits of sexual immorality that flood women when they indulge in fornication. Spirits of disease and death also invade these women when they indulge in fornication. These spirits enter into the women through their vagina. Demons love fellowship and love to move in gangs. Diseases like HIV and other viral diseases, which have killed millions of people, entered women and the human race through the vagina. Demons love to form gangs and groups. Demons of perversion, immorality, disease and death are constantly teaming up to invade women through their vaginas.

Keep your vagina zipped up tight, lest you become the habitation of devils! Watch out which vaginas you go exploring! You could receive a gang of demons from your partner! As you live longer, you will notice how some people are unable to recover from certain bouts of fornication for the rest of their lives. It is the power of evil spirits that have come to legally dwell in them and harass them.

## 6. THE DOOR OF THE ANUS

**For this reason God gave them over to degrading passions; for their women exchanged the natural function for that which is unnatural,**

**and in the same way also the men abandoned the natural function of the woman and burned in their desire toward one another, MEN WITH MEN COMMITTING INDECENT ACTS and receiving in their own persons the due penalty of their error.**

**And just as they did not see fit to acknowledge God any longer, God gave them over to a depraved mind, to do those things which are not proper,**

**Romans 1:26-28, NASB**

The anus is another hole in the body. Men commit indecent acts with each other by using the anus as a substitute for the vagina. This is clearly outlined in the scripture above. The anus exists for the passage of faeces. Unfortunately, the anus has been turned into an entrance for sexual organs. Some men have developed a loose anus which requires diapers to hold back their faeces.

The spirit of homosexuality and perversion enters the men through the act of forcing the penis through the anus. Homosexuality is a sin because the Bible says so. Several medical associations all over the world have come out clearly to say that no human being is born with that inclination. It is something that is acquired after birth.

The sin of homosexuality makes way for evil spirits to enter. The spiritual nature of homosexuality is seen by the strong desire that those who are involved in it have. It is one of the most debilitating and persuasive forces that can enter a man's life. The drive and need to commit fornication seems to be less than the need to continue in homosexuality. There is need for more compassion to be shown to those who have been involved in this life-changing activity.

The strong irresistible nature of this craving is recognised even by the law. The law recognises that a young person's life can be changed forever when he is molested by an adult. A person's life can be completely re-oriented by a powerful and unchanging force, after one homosexual contact. There are many adult men who trace the beginnings of their homosexual cravings to molestation in their childhood. Adults who destroy children's lives forever by penetrating their anuses are considered criminals. There is a great need for grace and compassion to help those who have been opened up to demons through their anuses.

It is not only spirits of homosexual cravings that enter through the anus. As usual, the gang of demons are ready to come into your body for fellowship. The HIV pandemic, which has slaughtered many people, came into the world through the homosexual spread of the HIV virus. Indeed, the anus has been the portal for the entrance of the spirits of death, abnormality and perversion.

# CHAPTER 24

# How You Can Tighten Security with the Armour of God

But let it be THE HIDDEN MAN of the heart, in that which is not corruptible, even the ornament of a meek and quiet spirit, which is in the sight of God of great price.

1 Peter 3:4

That he would grant you, according to the riches of his glory, to be strengthened with might by his Spirit in THE INNER MAN;

Ephesians 3:16

For I delight in the law of God after THE INWARD MAN:

Romans 7:22

In the spirit, you are actually shaped and seen as a man. You actually have a man's figure. The devils and angels see you spiritually as a man or woman. This is why the Bible describes the inner man, the inward man or the hidden man. You have a hidden man, an inner man or, if you prefer, an inward man.

It is this man that continues living after death as Jesus spoke of in the case of Lazarus and the rich man. Both the rich man and Lazarus were alive and able to communicate fully after death. Both the rich man, Lazarus and even Abraham, were alive and recognizable after death as men. You and I are indeed real men in the spirit and are seen clearly by devils, angels and even by God as such.

It is this inner man, hidden man or inward man that is also the target of devils. Hordes of demons are spying your inner man longingly and seeking a gap in your defences so that they can enter you and live happily ever after.

As a man you could be dressed or naked. The Laodiceans were described as Christians who were naked. Obviously this was not a physical nakedness because they were not even aware of their own nakedness. Their nakedness had to be pointed out to them.

**Because thou sayest, I am rich, and increased with goods, and have need of nothing; and KNOWEST NOT THAT THOU ART wretched, and miserable, and poor, and blind, and NAKED:**

**Revelation 3:17**

Apart from being clothed in the spirit, you can also be protected by armour. This armour gives you protection from flying invading demons that fill the atmosphere of the earth. Indeed, apostle Paul told all Christians to put on some armour. This is because there are demons that fly around like flocks of birds in the atmosphere.

There are demons that move around like swarms of insects and flies. These demons are seeking to find rest in human beings. If you relax, these DEVILS will invade you or your friends. If you joke with spiritual realities you may pay a very high price for it.

When you see a mad man, you may often wonder how his situation came to be. It is an age-old question. How do people become so exposed to devils? Why were devils able to turn a person into the living dead? Nearly everyone has a friend or someone they know that has been possessed by devils in a very frightening way. This reality makes us all want to protect ourselves from a possible exposure to demons.

The Bible clearly gives us the way to tighten security around us to be able to deflect many attacks of invading hordes of devils. The security of your soul, spirit and body can only be increased in the way revealed by the Word of God. You can defend yourself!

It is time to reduce all possible exposure to demons and invading devils. There are seven clear ways that increase your exposure to demonic hordes. You must fight to increase your security now! You must repel any invasions! You must defend yourself!

## Tighten Security with the Armour of God

1. **Staying with the truth and avoiding deception tightens the security of your spirit man against demons.** Lies and deception loosen the belt area of your spirit man and expose you in the spirit.

   Lies of any kind expose you to demonic invasions. Deception of any sort exposes you to demonic invasions. Self-deception of any kind exposes you to demonic invasions.

   **Stand therefore, HAVING YOUR LOINS GIRT ABOUT WITH TRUTH, and having on the breastplate of righteousness;**

   **Ephesians 6:14**

2.   **Practicing righteousness and avoiding sin tightens the security of your spirit man against demons.** Unrighteousness of any sort exposes the chest area of your spirit man to demonic hordes.

Sins of any kind expose you to demonic invasions. This means that any sin can lead demons that are flying by to descend and invade. If you are unlucky and there is a large horde of birds or insects in the area you can experience a terrible invasion.

**Stand therefore, having your loins girt about with truth, and having on THE BREASTPLATE OF RIGHTEOUSNESS;**

**Ephesians 6:14**

3.   **Emphasizing salvation tightens the security of your spirit man against demons.** Neglecting salvation exposes the head area of your spirit man to demonic invasion. Preaching and teaching about salvation tighten the security of the church.

Do not minimize the preaching and the value of salvation because that will expose your head to demons.

**And take THE HELMET OF SALVATION, and the sword of the Spirit, which is the word of God:**

**Ephesians 6:17**

4.   **Valuing the gospel and preaching the gospel tightens the security of your spirit man against demons.** Not preaching the gospel exposes the feet of your spirit man to demonic invasions.

**And your FEET SHOD WITH THE PREPARATION OF THE GOSPEL OF PEACE;**

**Ephesians 6:15**

5.   **Having faith and exercising faith tightens the security of your spirit man against demons.** Not having faith completely exposes you to devils. Faith in the calling! Faith in the invisible! Faith for Healing! Faith for prosperity!

**Above all, taking THE SHIELD OF FAITH, wherewith ye shall be able to quench all the fiery darts of the wicked.**

**Ephesians 6:16**

6.   **Using the word of God as the basis for everything tightens the security of your spirit man.** Every time you use the word of God you wave the sword of the Spirit and devils do not like that. That is why not using the word of God exposes you to demons. It is important to read the word of God, memorize the word of God, study the word of God and live your whole life according to the word of God. As you do this, the sword of the Spirit will be in motion and the security around your life will be heavily tightened.

**And take the helmet of salvation, and THE SWORD OF THE SPIRIT, WHICH IS THE WORD OF GOD:**

**Ephesians 6:17**

7.   **Praying always tightens the security of your spirit man against demons.** Not praying exposes everything about you to devils. This is why the apostle Paul gave us prayer as the final and overall thing we need to raise the security of our spirit man.

**Praying always with all prayer and supplication in the Spirit, and watching thereunto with all perseverance and supplication for all saints;**

**Ephesians 6:18**

# CHAPTER 25

# How You Can Block Attacks with the Armour of God

Put on the whole armour of God, that ye may be able to stand against THE WILES OF THE DEVIL.

Ephesians 6:11

I n this chapter, you want to go one step further. You want to do more than tighten security. You want to block out all attacks of satan against your life.

The wiles of the devil are the attacks of the most wicked creature in this world. Satan is so devious that it is not easy to see what he is doing. His wickedness against you is massive but you will only find out at the end.

Imagine lying in bed with a cobra sliding in silently under the bed sheets. You may even think you are receiving a massage as this deadly danger snuggles up to you. You may start dreaming about noodles and sausages as you gently caress the back of this evil cobra, which has slipped into your bed.

But God has given us the master revelation that will make it difficult for the tricks, traps and ambushes of the enemy to work.

## THE BELT OF TRUTH WILL BLOCK THE ATTACKS OF THE DEVIL

1.  **Do not entertain deception about the will of God in your life and you will effectively block the attacks, wiles and tricks of the devil.** You will block the wiles of the devil by blocking out lies, deception and untruths.

    And the Lord said, who shall persuade Ahab, that he may go up and fall at Ramothgilead? And one said on this manner, and another said on that manner. And there came forth a spirit, and stood before the Lord, and said, I will persuade him. And the Lord said unto him, wherewith? And he said, I will go forth, and I will be a lying spirit in the mouth of all his prophets. And he said, Thou shalt persuade him, and prevail also: go forth, and do so. Now therefore, behold, the Lord hath put a lying spirit in the mouth of all these thy prophets, and the Lord hath spoken evil concerning thee.

    1 Kings 22:20-23

2. **Do not entertain deception in your life about how beautiful or important you are and you will block the attacks of the devil.**

Again the word of the Lord came unto me, saying, Son of man, cause Jerusalem to know her abominations, And say, Thus saith the Lord God unto Jerusalem; Thy birth and thy nativity is of the land of Canaan; thy father was an Amorite, and thy mother an Hittite. And as for thy nativity, in the day thou wast born thy navel was not cut, neither wast thou washed in water to supple thee; thou wast not salted at all, nor swaddled at all. None eye pitied thee, to do any of these unto thee, to have compassion upon thee; but thou wast cast out in the open field, to the lothing of thy person, in the day that thou wast born.

And when I passed by thee, and saw thee polluted in thine own blood, I said unto thee when thou wast in thy blood, Live; yea, I said unto thee when thou wast in thy blood, Live. I have caused thee to multiply as the bud of the field, and thou hast increased and waxen great, and thou art come to excellent ornaments: thy breasts are fashioned, and thine hair is grown, whereas thou wast naked and bare. Now when I passed by thee, and looked upon thee, behold, thy time was the time of love; and I spread my skirt over thee, and covered thy nakedness: yea, I sware unto thee, and entered into a covenant with thee, saith the Lord God, and thou becamest mine. Then washed I thee with water; yea, I throughly washed away thy blood from thee, and I anointed thee with oil. I clothed thee also with broidered work, and shod thee with badgers' skin, and I girded thee about with fine linen, and I covered thee with silk.

I decked thee also with ornaments, and I put bracelets upon thy hands, and a chain on thy neck. And I put a jewel on thy forehead, and earrings in thine ears, and a beautiful crown upon thine head. Thus wast thou decked with gold and silver; and thy raiment was of fine linen, and silk, and broidered work; thou didst eat fine flour, and honey, and oil: and thou wast exceeding beautiful, and thou didst prosper into a kingdom. And thy renown went forth among the heathen for thy beauty: for it was perfect through my comeliness, which I had put upon thee, saith the Lord God.

But thou didst trust in thine own beauty, and playedst the harlot because of thy renown, and pouredst out thy fornications on every one that passed by; his it was.

Ezekiel 16:1-15

3. **Do not entertain deception in your life about the state of your church and you will block the sly attacks of the devil. Satan wants to destroy your church and bring you down to nothing.**

Be thou diligent to know the state of thy flocks, and look well to thy herds.

Proverbs 27:23

4. **Do not entertain deception in your life or be deceived about how strong you are spiritually and you will block out the attacks of the devil.**

Wherefore let him that thinketh he standeth take heed lest he fall.

1 Corinthians 10:12

5. **Do not entertain deception in your life about your relationship with the opposite sex and you will block out the attacks and wiles of the devil.**

And it came to pass afterward, that he loved a woman in the valley of Sorek, whose name was Delilah. And the lords of the Philistines came up unto her, and said unto her, Entice him, and see wherein his great strength lieth, and by what means we may prevail against him, that we may bind him to afflict him: and we will give thee every one of us eleven hundred pieces of silver.

And Delilah said to Samson, Tell me, I pray thee, wherein thy great strength lieth, and wherewith thou mightest be bound to afflict thee. And Samson said unto her, if they bind me with seven green withs that were never dried, then shall I be weak, and be as another man. Then the lords of the Philistines brought up to her seven green withs which had not been dried, and she bound him with them.

Now there were men lying in wait, abiding with her in the chamber. And she said unto him, The Philistines be upon thee, Samson. And he brake the withs, as a thread of tow is broken when it toucheth the fire. So his strength was not known. And Delilah said unto Samson, Behold, thou hast mocked me, and told me lies: now tell me, I pray thee, wherewith thou mightest be bound.

Judges 16:4-10

And she said unto him, How canst thou say, I love thee, when thine heart is not with me? Thou hast mocked me these three times, and hast not told me wherein thy great strength lieth. And it came to pass, when she pressed him daily with her words, and urged him, so that his soul was vexed unto death; That he told her all his heart, and said unto her, There hath not come a razor upon mine head; for I have been a Nazarite unto God from my mother's womb: if I be shaven, then my strength will go from me, and I shall become weak, and be like any other man.

And when Delilah saw that he had told her all his heart, she sent and called for the lords of the Philistines, saying, come up this once, for he hath shewed me all his heart. Then the lords of the Philistines came up unto her, and brought money in their hand. And she made him sleep upon her knees; and she called for a man, and she caused him to shave off the seven locks of his head; and she began to afflict him, and his strength went from him. And she said, The Philistines be upon thee, Samson. And he awoke out of his sleep, and said, I will go out as at other times before, and shake myself. And he wist not that the Lord was departed from him.

But the Philistines took him, and put out his eyes, and brought him down to Gaza, and bound him with fetters of brass; and he did grind in the prison house.

Judges 16:15-21

**6.    Do not entertain deception in your life about the importance of diligence and hard work and you will block out the attacks of the devil.**

How long will you slumber, O sluggard? When will you rise from your sleep? A little sleep, a little slumber, a little folding of the hands to sleep – so shall your poverty come on you like a prowler, and your need like an armed man.

Proverbs 6:9-11 (NKJV)

## THE BREASTPLATE OF RIGHTEOUSNESS WILL BLOCK THE WILES OF THE DEVIL

**1.    Do not commit fornication and you will block out the attacks of the devil.  Committing fornication breaks the breastplate and opens a gap for demons to enter your life.  You will block the wiles of the devil by blocking out sin and unrighteousness.**

And after these things I saw another angel come down from heaven, having great power; and the earth was lightened with his glory.  And he cried mightily with a strong voice, saying, Babylon the great is fallen, is fallen, and is become the habitation of devils, and the hold of every foul spirit, and a cage of every unclean and hateful bird.

For all nations have drunk of the wine of the wrath of her fornication, and the kings of the earth have committed fornication with her, and the merchants of the earth are waxed rich through the abundance of her delicacies.

Revelation 18:1-3

2. **Do not commit idolatry and you will block out the attacks of the devil. Committing idolatry breaks the breastplate and opens a gap for demons of destruction to enter your life.**

And the word of the Lord came unto me, saying, Son of man, these men have set up their idols in their heart, and put the stumblingblock of their iniquity before their face: should I be enquired of at all by them? Therefore speak unto them, and say unto them, Thus saith the Lord God; Every man of the house of Israel that setteth up his idols in his heart, and putteth the stumblingblock of his iniquity before his face, and cometh to the prophet; I the Lord will answer him that cometh according to the multitude of his idols; That I may take the house of Israel in their own heart, because they are all estranged from me through their idols.

Therefore say unto the house of Israel, Thus saith the Lord God; Repent, and turn yourselves from your idols; and turn away your faces from all your abominations. For every one of the house of Israel, or of the stranger that sojourneth in Israel, which separateth himself from me, and setteth up his idols in his heart, and putteth the stumblingblock of his iniquity before his face, and cometh to a prophet to enquire of him concerning me; I the Lord will answer him by myself: And I will set my face against that man, and will make him a sign and a proverb, and I will cut him off from the midst of my people; and ye shall know that I am the Lord. And if the prophet be deceived when he hath spoken a thing, I the Lord have deceived that prophet, and I will stretch out my hand upon him, and will destroy him from the midst of my people Israel.

Ezekiel 14:2-9

3.  **Do not get involved with witchcraft and the occult and you will block out attacks of the devil. Engaging in witchcraft and divination break the breastplate and opens a gap for demons of destruction to enter your life.**

The word of the Lord came unto me again, saying, also, thou son of man, appoint thee two ways, that the sword of the king of Babylon may come: both twain shall come forth out of one land: and choose thou a place, choose it at the head of the way to the city.

Appoint a way, that the sword may come to Rabbath of the Ammonites, and to Judah in Jerusalem the defenced. For the king of Babylon stood at the parting of the way, at the head of the two ways, to use divination: he made his arrows bright, he consulted with images, he looked in the liver. At his right hand was the divination for Jerusalem, to appoint captains, to open the mouth in the slaughter, to lift up the voice with shouting, to appoint battering rams against the gates, to cast a mount, and to build a fort.

And it shall be unto them as a false divination in their sight, to them that have sworn oaths: but he will call to remembrance the iniquity, that they may be taken.

Ezekiel 21:18-23

4.  **Do not commit homosexuality and you will block the attacks of the devil. Committing homosexuality breaks the breastplate and opens a gap for demons to enter your life.**

Wherefore God also gave them up to uncleanness through the lusts of their own hearts, to dishonour their own bodies between themselves: Who changed the truth of God into a lie, and worshipped and served the creature more than the Creator, who is blessed for ever. Amen.

For this cause God gave them up unto vile affections: for even their women did change the natural use into that which is against nature: And likewise also the men, leaving the natural use of the woman, burned in their lust one toward another; men with men working that which is unseemly, and receiving in themselves that recompence of their error which was meet.

Romans 1:24-27

5.   **Do not become proud and you will block the attacks the devil. Committing sins of pride breaks the breastplate and opens a gap for demons to enter your life.**

Pride goeth before destruction, and an haughty spirit before a fall.

Proverbs 16:18

6.   **Do not live in unforgiveness and you will block the attacks of the devil. Committing sins of unforgiveness breaks the breastplate and opens a gap for demons to enter your life.**

Therefore is the kingdom of heaven likened unto a certain king, which would take account of his servants. And when he had begun to reckon, one was brought unto him, which owed him ten thousand talents. But forasmuch as he had not to pay, his lord commanded him to be sold, and his wife, and children, and all that he had, and payment to be made.

The servant therefore fell down, and worshipped him, saying, Lord, have patience with me, and I will pay thee all. Then the lord of that servant was moved with compassion, and loosed him, and forgave him the debt. But the same servant went out, and found one of his fellowservants, which owed him an hundred pence: and he laid hands on him, and took him by the throat, saying, Pay me that thou owest. And his fellowservant fell down at his feet, and besought him, saying, Have patience with me, and I will pay thee all. And he would not: but went and cast him into prison, till he should pay the debt. So when his fellowservants saw what was done, they were very sorry, and came and told unto their lord all that was done. Then his lord, after that he had called him, said unto him, O thou wicked servant, I forgave thee all that debt, because thou desiredst me: Shouldest not thou also have had compassion on thy fellowservant, even as I had pity on thee? And his lord was wroth, and delivered him to THE TORMENTORS, till he should pay all that was due unto him. So likewise shall my heavenly Father do also unto you, if ye from your hearts forgive not every one his brother their trespasses.

Matthew 18:23-35

7.   **Do not be a wicked person and you will block attacks of the devil. Committing sins of wickedness breaks the breastplate and opens a gap for demons to enter your life.**

Be not over much wicked, neither be thou foolish: why shouldest thou die before thy time?

Ecclesiastes 7:17

8.   **Do not be self-righteous and over concerned about respectability and you will block out the attacks and wiles of the devil. Do not mete out unrighteous judgments. Committing sins of over righteousness, unrighteous judgment, self-respect, self-honour and being over dignified breaks the breastplate and opens a gap for demons to enter your life.**

Be not righteous over much; neither make thyself over wise: why shouldest thou destroy thyself?

Ecclesiastes 7:16

Let not mercy and truth forsake thee: bind them about thy neck; write them upon the table of thine heart: So shalt thou find favour and good understanding in the sight of God and man.

Proverbs 3:3-4

9.  **Do not be disobedient and you will block attacks of the devil. Committing the sin of disobedience breaks the breastplate and opens a gap for demons to enter your life.**

But it shall come to pass, if thou wilt not hearken unto the voice of the Lord thy God, to observe to do all his commandments and his statutes which I command thee this day; that all these curses shall come upon thee, and overtake thee: Cursed shalt thou be in the city, and cursed shalt thou be in the field. Cursed shall be thy basket and thy store. Cursed shall be the fruit of thy body, and the fruit of thy land, the increase of thy kine, and the flocks of thy sheep. Cursed shalt thou be when thou comest in, and cursed shalt thou be when thou goest out. The Lord shall send upon thee cursing, vexation, and rebuke, in all that thou settest thine hand unto for to do, until thou be destroyed, and until thou perish quickly; because of the wickedness of thy doings, whereby thou hast forsaken me.

Deuteronomy 28:15-20

## THE PREACHING OF THE GOSPEL WILL BLOCK OUT THE TRICKS OF THE DEVIL

1.  **Do not stop preaching the gospel and you will block the attacks and wiles of the devil. Not preaching the gospel and not being prepared with the gospel opens a gap in our armour and allows demons of lack and need to invade.**

But seek ye first the kingdom of God, and his righteousness; and all these things shall be added unto you.

Matthew 6:33

2.    **Do not stop preaching the gospel and you will block out the attacks of the devil.  Not preaching the gospel and not being prepared with the gospel opens a gap in your armour and allows demons of lukewarmness into your life.**

I know thy works, that thou art neither cold nor hot: I would thou wert cold or hot. So then because thou art lukewarm, and neither cold nor hot, I will spue thee out of my mouth.

Revelation 3:15-16

3.    **Do not stop preaching the gospel and you will block out the attacks of the devil.  Not preaching the gospel and not being prepared with the gospel opens a gap in the armour and allows demons of woes and problems into your life.**

For though I preach the gospel, I have nothing to glory of: for necessity is laid upon me; yea, WOE IS UNTO ME, IF I PREACH NOT the gospel!

1 Corinthians 9:16

4.    **Do not stop preaching the gospel and you will block out the attacks and wiles of the devil.  Not preaching the gospel and not being prepared with the gospel opens a gap in your armour and allows demons that cancel church growth to invade.**

The scriptures below show how preaching the gospel opens the door for church growth.  Many churches are struggling with demons of church decline sitting at the door.  Their churches are reducing and getting smaller every day.  They do not understand why satan seems to have stolen the entire congregation, leaving them with so few people.

And with many other words did he testify and exhort, saying, Save yourselves from this untoward generation.

Then they that gladly received his word were baptized: and the same day THERE WERE ADDED UNTO THEM ABOUT THREE THOUSAND SOULS.

Acts 2:40-42

Howbeit MANY OF THEM WHICH HEARD THE WORD BELIEVED; and THE NUMBER of the men WAS ABOUT FIVE THOUSAND.

Acts 4:4

And believers were the more added to the Lord, MULTITUDES both of men and women.

Acts 5:14

Now when the congregation was broken up, many of the Jews and religious proselytes followed Paul and Barnabas: who, speaking to them, persuaded them to continue in the grace of God.

And THE NEXT SABBATH DAY CAME almost THE WHOLE CITY TOGETHER TO HEAR THE WORD OF GOD.

Acts 13:43-44

## THE SHIELD OF FAITH WILL BLOCK THE TRICKS OF THE DEVIL

1. **Do not stop having faith and you will block out the attacks of the devil. Not having faith opens a gap in your armour and allows demons of poverty into your life.** Exercising faith releases prosperity and blocks poverty. It is important to believe all the scriptures of prosperity that are in the Bible.

Beloved, I wish above all things that thou mayest prosper and be in health, even as thy soul prospereth.

3 John 2

2.  **Do not stop having faith and you will block out the attacks of the devil. Not having faith opens a gap in your armour and allows demons of difficulty and pain into your life.** Exercising faith releases prosperity and pleasure into your life.

If they obey and serve him, they shall spend their days in prosperity, and their years in pleasures.

Job 36:11

3.  **Do not stop having faith and you will block out the attacks of the devil. Not having faith opens a gap in your armour and allows demons of sickness into your life.** Exercising faith releases health and blocks sicknesses in your life.

Beloved, I wish above all things that thou mayest prosper and be in health, even as thy soul prospereth.

3 John 2

4.  **Do not stop having faith and you will block out the attacks of the devil. Not having faith opens a gap in your armour and allows demons of difficulty into your life.** Exercising faith opens the door for your desires to be met.

Therefore I say unto you, what things soever ye desire, when ye pray, believe that ye receive them, and ye shall have them.

Mark 11:24

5.  **Do not stop having faith and you will block out the attacks of the devil. Not having faith opens a gap in your armour and allows demons of great problems and mountains to stay in your life.** Exercising faith moves mountains and blocks the activities of demons of insurmountable problems.

For verily I say unto you, That whosoever shall say unto this mountain, Be thou removed, and be thou cast into the sea; and shall not doubt in his heart, but shall believe that those things which he saith shall come to pass; he shall have whatsoever he saith.

Mark 11:23

6.  **Do not stop having faith and you will block out the attacks of the devil.  Not having faith opens a gap in your armour and allows demons of shipwreck into your life.**  Exercising faith releases your desires and blocks utter destruction in your life.  Satan would love to actually destroy you.  A shipwreck speaks of utter destruction.

Holding faith, and a good conscience; which some having put away concerning faith have made shipwreck:

1 Timothy 1:19

### THE HELMET OF SALVATION WILL BLOCK THE ATTACKS OF THE DEVIL

**Setting aside the foundations of salvation opens a gap in your armour and allows demons into your life.**  You can block demons with the helmet of salvation.  You will open the door to demons through a lack of preaching about salvation in the church and by a devaluation of the concept of salvation in the church. Emphasizing the foundations of salvation gives power to the Christian church and blocks evil spirits from entering our lives. Salvation is a foundation of our Christian lives.

If the foundations be destroyed, what can the righteous do?

Psalms 11:3

1.  **Do not stop talking about salvation and you will block out the attacks of the devil.  Setting aside the foundations of salvation opens a gap in your armour and allows demons of materialism and earthly-**

**mindedness into your life.** Exercising faith releases your desires and blocks negative things in your life.

Set your affection on things above, not on things on the earth. For ye are dead, and your life is hid with Christ in God.

Colossians 3:2-3

2.  **Do not stop talking about salvation and you will block out the attacks of the devil. Setting aside the foundations of salvation opens a gap in your armour and allows demons of vain jangling into your life.** Emphasizing the foundations of salvation gives you power as a Christians and blocks evil spirits from entering your life.

    Now the end of the commandment is charity out of a pure heart, and of a good conscience, and of faith unfeigned: From which some having swerved have turned aside unto vain jangling;

1 Timothy 1:5-6

3.  **Do not stop talking about salvation and you will block out the attacks of the devil. Setting aside the foundations of salvation opens a gap in your armour and allows demons of unfaithfulness and disloyalty into your life.** Emphasizing the foundations of salvation gives you power as a Christians and blocks evil spirits from entering your life.

    According to the glorious gospel of the blessed God, which was committed to my trust. And I thank Christ Jesus our Lord, who hath enabled me, for that he counted me faithful, putting me into the ministry;

1 Timothy 1:11-12

## THE SWORD OF THE SPIRIT WILL BLOCK
## THE ATTACKS OF THE DEVIL

1.  **Do not stop using the word of God as the basis for everything and you will block out the attacks of the devil. Not using the sword of the Spirit opens a gap in your armour and allows *demons of deceptive fleshly temptation* into your life.** You can block demons with the sword of the Spirit. You will open the door to demons by setting aside the word of God.

And the devil said unto him, if thou be the Son of God, COMMAND THIS STONE THAT IT BE MADE BREAD. And Jesus answered him, saying, it is written, that man shall not live by bread alone, but by every word of God.

Luke 4:3-4

2.  **Do not stop using the word of God as the basis for everything and you will block out the attacks of the devil. Not using the sword of the Spirit opens a gap in your armour and allows *demons of deceptive and deadly short cuts* into your life.**

And the devil, taking him up into an high mountain, shewed unto him all the kingdoms of the world in a moment of time. And the devil said unto him, All this power will I give thee, and the glory of them: for that is delivered unto me; and to whomsoever I will I give it. IF THOU THEREFORE WILT WORSHIP ME, ALL SHALL BE THINE. And Jesus answered and said unto him, Get thee behind me, Satan: for it is written, Thou shalt worship the Lord thy God, and him only shalt thou serve.

Luke 4:5-8

3.  **Do not stop using the word of God as the basis for everything and you will block out the attacks of the devil. Not using the sword of the Spirit opens a gap in your armour and allows *deceptive demons of misuse of power* into your life.**

200

And he brought him to Jerusalem, and set him on a pinnacle of the temple, and said unto him, If thou be the Son of God, cast thyself down from hence: For it is written, He shall give his angels charge over thee, to keep thee: And in their hands they shall bear thee up, lest at any time thou dash thy foot against a stone. And Jesus answering said unto him, It is said, Thou shalt not tempt the Lord thy God.

Luke 4:9-12

## "PRAYING ALWAYS" WILL BLOCK THE ATTACKS OF THE DEVIL

1. **Do not stop "praying always" and you will block out the attacks of the devil. Not praying always opens a gap in your armour and allows wicked spirits in high places to work against you and oppose your mission. You can block demons with prayer.** You will open the door to demons by prayerlessness.

And he said unto me, O Daniel, a man greatly beloved, understand the words that I speak unto thee, and stand upright: for unto thee am I now sent. And when he had spoken this word unto me, I stood trembling. Then said he unto me, Fear not, Daniel: for from the first day that thou didst set thine heart to understand, and to chasten thyself before thy God, THY WORDS WERE HEARD, AND I AM COME FOR THY WORDS.

But THE PRINCE OF THE KINGDOM OF PERSIA WITHSTOOD ME one and twenty days: but, lo, Michael, one of the chief princes, came to help me; and I remained there with the kings of Persia. Now I am come to make thee understand what shall befall thy people in the latter days: for yet the vision is for many days. And when he had spoken such words unto me, I set my face toward the ground, and I became dumb. And, behold, one like the similitude of the sons of men touched my lips: then

I opened my mouth, and spake, and said unto him that stood before me, O my lord, by the vision my sorrows are turned upon me, and I have retained no strength. For how can the servant of this my lord talk with this my lord? For as for me, straightway there remained no strength in me, neither is there breath left in me. Then there came again and touched me one like the appearance of a man, and he strengthened me, And said, O man greatly beloved, fear not: peace be unto thee, be strong, yea, be strong. And when he had spoken unto me, I was strengthened, and said, let my lord speak; for thou hast strengthened me.

Daniel 10:11-19

2.  **Do not stop "praying always" and you will block out the attacks of the devil. Not praying always opens a gap in your armour and allows wicked spirits in high places to steal your understanding.**

And he said unto me, O Daniel, a man greatly beloved, understand the words that I speak unto thee, and stand upright: for unto thee am I now sent. And when he had spoken this word unto me, I stood trembling. Then said he unto me, Fear not, Daniel: for from the first day that thou didst set thine heart to understand, and to chasten thyself before thy God, THY WORDS WERE HEARD, AND I AM COME FOR THY WORDS.

But the prince of the kingdom of Persia withstood me one and twenty days: but, lo, Michael, one of the chief princes, came to help me; and I remained there with the kings of Persia. Now I AM COME TO MAKE THEE UNDERSTAND what shall befall thy people in the latter days: for yet the vision is for many days. And when he had spoken such words unto me, I set my face toward the ground, and I became dumb. And, behold, one like the similitude of the sons of men touched my lips: then I opened my mouth, and spake, and said unto him that stood before me, O my lord, by the vision my sorrows are turned upon me, and I have retained no strength. For how can the servant of this my lord talk with this my lord? for as for me, straightway there remained no strength in me, neither is there breath left in me. Then there came again and touched me one like the appearance of a man, and he strengthened me, And said, O man greatly beloved, fear not: peace be unto thee, be strong, yea, be strong. And when he had spoken unto me, I was strengthened, and said, let my lord speak; for thou hast strengthened me.

Daniel 10:11-19

3.  **Do not stop "praying always" and you will block out the attacks and wiles of the devil. Not praying always opens a gap in your armour and allows wicked spirits in high places to steal your strength in ministry.**

And he said unto me, O Daniel, a man greatly beloved, understand the words that I speak unto thee, and stand upright: for unto thee am I now sent. And when he had spoken this word unto me, I stood trembling. Then said he unto me, Fear not, Daniel: for from the first day that thou didst set thine heart to understand, and to chasten thyself before thy God, THY WORDS WERE HEARD, AND I AM COME FOR THY WORDS.

But the prince of the kingdom of Persia withstood me one and twenty days: but, lo, Michael, one of the chief princes, came to help me; and I remained there with the kings of Persia. Now I am come to make thee understand what shall befall thy people in the latter days: for yet the vision is for many days. And when he had spoken such words unto me, I set my face toward the ground, and I became dumb. And, behold, one like the similitude of the sons of men touched my lips: then I opened my mouth, and spake, and said unto him that stood before me, O my lord, by the vision my sorrows are turned upon me, and I have retained no strength. For how can the servant of this my lord talk with this my lord? for as for me, straightway there remained no strength in me, neither is there breath left in me. THEN THERE CAME AGAIN AND TOUCHED ME ONE LIKE THE APPEARANCE OF A MAN, AND HE STRENGTHENED ME, And said, O man greatly beloved, fear not: peace be unto thee, be strong, yea, be strong. And when he had spoken unto me, I WAS STRENGTHENED, AND SAID, LET MY LORD SPEAK; FOR THOU HAST STRENGTHENED ME.

Daniel 10:11-19

4.  **Do not stop "praying always" and you will block out the attacks of the devil. Not praying opens a gap in your armour and allows wicked spirits in high places to steal your peace in ministry.**

And he said unto me, O Daniel, a man greatly beloved, understand the words that I speak unto thee, and stand upright: for unto thee am I now sent. And when he had spoken this word unto me, I stood trembling. Then said he unto me, Fear not, Daniel: for from the first day that thou didst set thine heart to understand, and to chasten thyself before thy God, THY WORDS WERE HEARD, AND I AM COME FOR THY WORDS.

But the prince of the kingdom of Persia withstood me one and twenty days: but, lo, Michael, one of the chief princes, came to help me; and I remained there with the kings of Persia. Now I am come to make thee understand what shall befall thy people in the latter days: for yet the vision is for many days. And when he had spoken such words unto me, I set my face toward the ground, and I became dumb. And, behold, one like the similitude of the sons of men touched my lips: then I opened my mouth, and spake, and said unto him that stood before me, O my lord, by the vision my sorrows are turned upon me, and I have retained no strength. For how can the servant of this my lord talk with this my lord? for as for me, straightway there remained no strength in me, neither is there breath left in me. Then there came again and touched me one like the appearance of a man, and he strengthened me, AND SAID, O MAN GREATLY BELOVED, FEAR NOT: PEACE BE UNTO THEE, be strong, yea, be strong. And when he had spoken unto me, I was strengthened, and said, let my lord speak; for thou hast strengthened me.

Daniel 10:11-19

5. **Do not stop "praying always" and you will block out the attacks of the devil. Not praying always opens a gap in your armour and allows evil spirits of confusion, lack of peace, lack of godliness and dishonesty to enter your life.**

I exhort therefore, that, first of all, supplications, prayers, intercessions, and giving of thanks, be made for all men; For kings, and for all that are in authority; that we may lead a quiet and peaceable life in all godliness and honesty.

1 Timothy 2:1-2

# CHAPTER 26

# How to Avoid Becoming A Habitation of Devils

And he cried mightily with a strong voice, saying,
Babylon the great is fallen, is fallen, and is become
THE HABITATION OF DEVILS, and the hold of
every foul spirit, and a cage of every unclean and
hateful bird.

Revelation 18:2

The main aim of unclean spirits and hybrid creatures is to occupy you. Once they are in you, you are declared fallen. Babylon was declared fallen because she had become the habitation, the cage and the container of these evil spirits.

Once you are a cage, a hold or a habitation of these evil spirits, you are declared fallen. Your fight as a Christian is to protect your entry points so that these creatures will not be able to come into you.

There are several things that evil spirits utterly dislike. Each time you do any of these things, you greatly terrorise, intimidate, frighten, confuse and dispel evil spirits. Take note of each of these activities. If you practice them, you will greatly intimidate and scatter evil entities that are sent to destroy you. Evil spirits will not feel comfortable in your company if you do these things. If you do these things, evil spirits will think twice about attacking you.

## 1.    Avoid becoming a habitation of devils by being filled with good things.

Evil spirits wish to declare you as their established home and address. Babylon was completely destroyed when she became the cage of evil spirits. To fall, according to Revelation 18:2 is to have become the habitation and the home of evil spirits.

Your duty is to fill your life with the good things of the Word, the Holy Spirit and the power of God. Nature abhors a vacuum. When the evil spirits come back and find the house empty, they immediately rush in to fill the space. This is why satan does not want you to listen to the Word of God. This is why satan does not want you to read your Bible and other Christian books. This is why satan does not want you to pray in tongues and be filled with the Spirit. Satan wants you to be an empty head and an empty house so he can invade you and fill you.

An empty house is a great and welcoming home to evil spirits and evil creatures. There are many people walking around with hateful and unclean birds living in them. The fall of Babylon was caused by the successful invasion of it by evil spirits, foul spirits and unclean birds.

Do you want to fall? Do you want to be occupied by evil spirits? Of course not! You will never be occupied by demons! You will never be called an occupied territory of the dark kingdom!

I am sure you understand why God wants us to be filled with the Spirit.

**And Moses said unto the children of Israel, See, the Lord hath called by name Bezaleel the son of Uri, the son of Hur, of the tribe of Judah;**

**And he hath FILLED HIM WITH THE SPIRIT OF GOD, in wisdom, in understanding, and in knowledge, and in all manner of workmanship;**

**Exodus 35:30-31**

**And when they had prayed, the place was shaken where they were assembled together; and they were all FILLED WITH THE HOLY GHOST, and they spake the word of God with boldness.**

**Acts 4:31**

I am sure you understand why God wants us to be filled with the Word of God.

**LET THE WORD OF CHRIST DWELL IN YOU RICHLY in all wisdom; teaching and admonishing one another in psalms and hymns and spiritual songs, singing with grace in your hearts to the Lord.**

**Colossians 3:16**

I am sure you understand why God wants us to be filled with the knowledge of God.

**For the earth shall be FILLED WITH the KNOWLEDGE of the glory of the Lord, as the waters cover the sea.**

**Habakkuk 2:14**

I am sure you understand why God wants us to be filled with the knowledge of His will.

ʼ  **For this cause we also, since the day we heard it, do not cease to pray for you, and to desire that ye might be FILLED WITH the KNOWLEDGE of his will in all wisdom and spiritual understanding;**

**Colossians 1:9**

I am sure you understand why God wants us to be filled with the fullness of God.

**And to know the love of Christ, which passeth knowledge, that ye might be FILLED WITH ALL THE FULNESS OF GOD.**

**Ephesians 3:19**

These are the very things that keep you from becoming the habitation of devils.

2.  **Avoid becoming a habitation of devils by surrounding yourself with the preaching of the Word and it will drive away devils.  Demons do not like the preaching of the Word.**

And they went into Capernaum; and straightway on the Sabbath day he entered into the synagogue, and taught. And they were astonished at his doctrine: for he taught them as one that had authority, and not as the scribes.

And there was in their synagogue a man with an unclean spirit; and he cried out, Saying, LET US ALONE; what have we to do with thee, thou Jesus of Nazareth? Art thou come to destroy us? I know thee who thou art, the Holy

One of God. And Jesus rebuked him, saying, Hold thy peace, and come out of him.

And when the unclean spirit had torn him, and cried with a loud voice, he came out of him.

*Mark 1:21-26*

You will notice that the demons in the man shouted, "Leave us alone". Jesus had not rebuked the devil; neither had he cast the devil out. Jesus was only teaching the scripture. But the Word of God is a sharp sword in the spirit. Every time the Word of God is going forth, a sword is flying through the air, cutting away and attacking strongholds. This is why Christians who listen to the teaching and preaching of the Word of God become free of evil spirits over time. They may never be prayed for. They may never have demons cast out of them. But the evil spirits are forced to leave because of the two-edged swords that are constantly thrown at them. Would you like to live in a place where swords are flying all around you every day? Certainly not! Demons do not want to live in someone who allows the sword of the Spirit to fly through him every day and every night.

This is why people who listen to messages are changed dramatically. Evil spirits are driven out of them by the Word of God. The Word of God is also a light that shines into the darkness of our lives. All the evil creatures that dwell in darkness do not like light being shed on them and on their activities.

You may make fun of churches that do not conduct deliverance sessions or shout in tongues. You may make fun of churches that do not have demon casting church services. You may say, "These churches have no power. They only teach the Word." But that is your mistake. Teaching the Word is a very powerful tool for intimidating, terrorising, tormenting and repelling evil spirits. Follow the example of Jesus and teach the Word of God. The evil powers in your church members are being broken every day as the Word comes forth.

3.   **Avoid becoming a habitation of devils by receiving prophetic declarations and it will drive away devils. Demons do not like prophetic declarations of faith.**

And he was teaching in one of the synagogues on the Sabbath.

And, behold, there was a woman which had a spirit of infirmity eighteen years, and was bowed together, and could in no wise lift up herself.

And WHEN JESUS SAW HER, HE CALLED HER TO HIM, AND SAID UNTO HER, WOMAN, THOU ART LOOSED FROM THINE INFIRMITY.

And he laid his hands on her: and immediately she was made straight, and glorified God.

Luke 13:10-13

Jesus ministered to this woman who was bound with the spirit of infirmity for eighteen years. How exactly did He minister to her? He spoke a word to her. This was a word of power, faith and prophecy. He was inspired by the Holy Spirit to say those words. When a word of faith is spoken, it has creative power. Jesus said, "Whosoever shall say to a mountain, 'be thou removed and be thou cast into the sea' and shall not doubt, he shall have what he says."

In other words, a word spoken in faith has amazing power if it is received with faith.

Demons do not like such declarations.

Demons absolutely hate to hear things like, "Be healed! Be blessed! Be delivered! You are blessed! Receive your miracle! Rise and be healed! You will never be found at the same spot again by next year!"

These are powerful declarations of faith. Each of these declarations can cause an evil spirit to move out of you as it did in the case of the woman who had been bent over for eighteen years. If you are a pastor, learn to speak powerful faith-filled blessings over your people. Your words will come to pass and demons will lose their control over your members.

4.  **Avoid becoming a habitation of devils by having quality hands laid on you and it will drive away devils. Demons do not like hands being laid on people.**

> And he was teaching in one of the synagogues on the Sabbath.
>
> And, behold, there was a woman which had A SPIRIT OF INFIRMITY eighteen years, and was bowed together, and could in no wise lift up herself.
>
> And when Jesus saw her, he called her to him, and said unto her, woman, thou art loosed from thine infirmity.
>
> And HE LAID HIS HANDS ON HER: AND IMMEDIATELY SHE WAS MADE STRAIGHT, and glorified God.
>
> Luke 13:10-13

When Jesus laid hands on the woman, the evil spirit did not feel comfortable to stay in her any longer. Evil spirits do not like hands being laid on people because the laying on of hands causes the transmission of God's power. The laying on of hands is a biblical principle for the transmission of power from one person to another. This is why the devil does not like ministers who lay hands on people. Every time hands are being laid on you, remember that power is being transmitted into you and evil spirits are being dislodged.

5.  **Avoid becoming a habitation of devils by praying without ceasing and it will drive away devils. Demons do not like prayer.**

> Then came the disciples to Jesus apart, and said, why could not we cast him out?
>
> And Jesus said unto them, Because of your unbelief: for verily I say unto you, If ye have faith as a grain of mustard seed, ye shall say unto this mountain, Remove hence to yonder place; and it shall remove; and nothing shall be

impossible unto you. Howbeit THIS KIND GOETH NOT OUT BUT BY PRAYER and fasting.

Matthew 17:19-21

The scripture above is very clear about devils being affected greatly by prayer and fasting. Prayer is so important in your fight against devils. A prayerless Christian is a welcoming hotel for roaming evil spirits. When evil spirits spot Christians who talk a lot but do not pray, they become excited at the possibility of renting a room right there. When you walk about in your room and pray, you are disorienting and intimidating evil creatures that may be hovering in your area. Evil spirits sitting on the branches of the tree outside your room will move further away to the next house where there is no one who speaks in tongues. Remember that evil spirits are constantly roaming and searching for a place to rest, a place to inhabit and a place to dominate.

Evil spirits, like animals, are territorial. That is why they are called principalities. They dominate areas. This is why different areas have different characteristics and different evils. They move away from dangerous prayerful zones into welcoming prayerless areas.

6.  **Avoid becoming a habitation of devils by fasting continuously and it will drive away devils. Demons do not like fasting.**

And Jesus rebuked the devil; and he departed out of him: and the child was cured from that very hour. Then came the disciples to Jesus apart, and said, why could not we cast him out? And Jesus said unto them, Because of your unbelief: for verily I say unto you, If ye have faith as a grain of mustard seed, ye shall say unto this mountain, Remove hence to yonder place; and it shall remove; and nothing shall be impossible unto you.

Howbeit this kind goeth not out but by prayer and FASTING.

Matthew 17:18-21

213

Fasting subdues the flesh. Evil spirits feed on the flesh and love to stimulate the flesh of Christians constantly. Whenever Christians fast, they subdue the flesh and make it uninteresting for evil spirits to feed on. Demon activity is greatly reduced by fasting. All works of the flesh are put on hold until the fast is over. Sometimes Christians are attacked even more after the fast is over. This is often a rebound attack of starved evil spirits who are trying to re-establish their weakened positions.

You are free from every demonic power and influence! You are declared a master of magicians, devils, witches and wizards by the power of the Holy Spirit and by the power of the blood of Jesus.